History
TODAY

James Montgomery
A man for all people

Paul S Taylor

DayOne

ISBN 978–1–84625–209–9

British Library Cataloguing in Publication Data available

Unless otherwise indicated, Scripture quotations are from the **New King James Version (NKJV)®**. Copyright © 1982 by Thomas Nelson, Inc. Used by permission. All rights reserved.

Published by Day One Publications
Ryelands Road, Leominster, HR6 8NZ
☎ 01568 613 740 FAX 01568 611 473
email—sales@dayone.co.uk
web site—www.dayone.co.uk
North American—e-mail—sales@dayonebookstore.com
North American—web site—www.dayonebookstore.com

Cover design by Wayne McMaster
Printed by Orchard Press Cheltenham Ltd, Tewkesbury

James Montgomery is one of our great hymn-writers, deservedly standing alongside Charles Wesley and Isaac Watts. In his day, he was acclaimed a great poet and social reformer. A successful businessman, he was a publisher, newspaper proprietor and editor. Above all else, he was a man of steadfast Christian faith.

There has long been a need for a modern assessment of Montgomery's life and achievements. Paul Taylor's book fills the gap admirably. He presents a balanced and lively study of this remarkable man. The book is a valuable reference work, but it is more than this: it is an eminently readable story of the influences that made Montgomery and of the impact he had upon local and national events of the early 19th century.

Montgomery lives on in his hymns. Paul Taylor convinces us that, even without the hymns, there is a fascinating story to be told.

George Tolley, Canon Emeritus of Sheffield Cathedral and former Principal of Sheffield City Polytechnic, UK

I enjoyed reading Paul Taylor's book James Montgomery: A Man for All People. *The extensive bibliography indicates wide reading around the subject, and the author's appreciation of the man and his works comes through clearly.*

Although I had known of and read about James Montgomery since my days at Fulneck School, it was a pleasure to see this easy-to-read account of his life and work. We find that, like many in the Moravian Church, Montgomery was a traveller and worked hard on both missionary and Bible tours. His work as a social reformer—his involvement in campaigns against slavery and the use of chimney-sweep boys—is also recorded. The appendices are helpful in providing additional background information, and the chapter on Montgomery's hymns is particularly interesting.

This volume will give a general introduction to the 'man for all people'; as Montgomery himself says, 'This is the way God's gifts to use, first enjoy and then diffuse.'

Bishop John McOwat, the Moravian Church, UK

Commendations

The memorial statue to James Montgomery has been dusted down and re-sited adjacent to Sheffield Cathedral. But who was he, and what were his achievements? Paul Taylor has helpfully provided the answer in this new and long-overdue biography. Poet, hymn-writer, journalist, zealous Christian and agitator for good causes, Montgomery should be better known. Twice committed to prison for comments on sensitive political issues, he has been let loose by Taylor to edify us.

Paul E. G. Cook, pastor, preacher and writer, UK

Contents

FOREWORD **6**

PREFACE **7**

ACKNOWLEDGEMENTS **10**

1 UNFOLDING POWERS **12**

2 THE WANDERER **30**

3 *THE REGISTER* AND *THE IRIS* **41**

4 WIDE HORIZONS **55**

5 CAUSES AND EFFECTS **76**

6 HYMNS OF GLORY, SONGS OF PRAISE **90**

APPENDIX 1: THE BARD OF SHEFFIELD: THE LONGER POEMS **118**

APPENDIX 2: CHRONOLOGICAL PROFILE **123**

APPENDIX 3: THE WORLD OF JAMES MONTGOMERY **125**

SELECT BIBLIOGRAPHY **128**

INDEX OF PLACES **130**

INDEX OF NAMES **133**

Foreword

Although James Montgomery was one of our most respected hymn-writers, very little material has been written with regard to his life and work. I am therefore grateful to Paul Taylor for rectifying this omission. This book will enhance the library of any true student of hymnology.

I particularly appreciate the opportunity of writing this Foreword as, coming from South Yorkshire, I have had an interest in this remarkable character for many years. It began in the early 1950s when I attended Montgomery Hall in Sheffield to take examinations for piano playing and also for Sunday-school presentations. At that time I was unaware of the link between the hall and the hymn-writer. It was in 1976, shortly after I became Director of Day One Christian Ministries, that my interest in Montgomery developed. I was invited to address a meeting held in the Montgomery Hall, and a local historian informed me that the hall had been built in memory of James Montgomery. From that time on, there was no looking back.

As I had an interest in hymnology, I began to read carefully some of the 400 hymns Montgomery had written. Without doubt he was one of our greatest poets. His use of the English language and his deep spiritual insight have made his hymns of real benefit to the worshipper. His breadth of biblical knowledge is encompassed in the wide selection of hymns he wrote covering the nativity, prayer, the Lord's Supper and the Second Coming of our Lord, to name just a few of the themes Montgomery covered. He also gave us a wide selection of hymns to enable believers to enter the very presence of God and enjoy the benefits of being there. James Montgomery was a godly man who used the gifts God had entrusted to him, and the results are still with us today.

In this book, Paul Taylor writes with warmth and great regard for a man who deserves to be known far beyond the boundaries of South Yorkshire. From reading this history, you will discover that Montgomery stands alongside Wesley and Watts as one of our greatest hymn-writers. I have no hesitation in commending the book and its subject.

John Roberts
General Director, Day One Christian Ministries, UK

Since the monumental work of John Holland and James Everett, who published a seven-volume life of James Montgomery at about the time of his death in 1854 (*Memoirs of the Life and Writings of James Montgomery*; henceforth *Memoirs*), there has been no serious attempt, as far as I know, to write a biography of one of England's greatest Christian hymn-writers. This book seeks to rectify the omission and to present a popular but serious evaluation of Montgomery's varied life.

Both James Montgomery and his missionary parents were influenced by John Cennick, the 18th-century evangelist who had associated with Whitefield and the Wesleys and had been involved in the Moravian settlements at Gracehill in the north of Ireland and at Fulneck in what is now West Yorkshire. Both these settlements played a formative part in the youth of James Montgomery. The story of John Cennick is told in the recently published biography, *Bold as a Lion: John Cennick, Moravian Evangelist* (Peter Gentry and Paul Taylor; Leicester: Life Publications, 2007).

The Town Hall in Wath-on-Dearne, South Yorkshire, where I worked for several years, faces Montgomery Road. While I was there, in the early 1950s, there was also an imposing public building named Montgomery Hall. I showed little interest then in Christians or their hymns, and no one explained to me the significance of the name Montgomery. When James Montgomery arrived at Wath-on-Dearne in 1789, this small town was then little more than a hamlet on the banks of the river Dearne, but it was to become an important staging-post in the journey of Montgomery's early life.

I also worked for a time in the city of Sheffield, which has a famous Victorian Town Hall, at the side of which, in Surrey Street, stands Montgomery Hall, now the office of the Sheffield Christian Education Council and the home of some Montgomery archives. How James Montgomery came to Wath-on-Dearne and Sheffield is a story of God's providential ways, full of interest, drama, highs and lows, victories and defeats, which led to the unusual ministry that belonged uniquely to James Montgomery.

Montgomery was a devout Christian gentleman, a man with a spirituality nurtured in his evangelical Moravian background, a heritage of faith to which he returned after a period of wandering in the wilderness of the secular world. His love of the Scriptures adorns all his well-known hymns, and his devotion to the Lord Jesus Christ permeated all his work—especially after his experience of restoration.

He inherited a disposition prone to periods of melancholy and occasional depression, similar to but not as acute as that experienced by William Cowper of Olney. As his story unfolds, it will not be difficult to understand his dark times.

Montgomery was a man who loved people, even those who were not always sympathetic to his work and ways. Many of his letters shine with a high regard for people who did not share his views. The affectionate nature with which he was endowed makes it all the more remarkable that he never married. There was one occasion when he enigmatically referred to a 'marriage', but it is certain that he had no wife.

He was naturally gifted with unusual poetic and musical talents. Perhaps he fell a little short of the greatest poets, and he was never a musical genius, but he was remarkably talented for all that. One author wrote of Montgomery's hymns that they had 'an earnestness, a fervour of piety, and an unmistakable sincerity which goes straight to the heart'.

Montgomery's foundation doctrines were thoroughly evangelical, as can be seen from all his Christian writings. He became involved in many activities which helped to alleviate some of the desperate social problems of Sheffield, his adopted city, in the 19th century.

The occasion of his funeral in 1854 brought that city to a virtual standstill. Such was his standing and popularity that he was honoured on that day by his fellow citizens in a way not previously shown to any other public figure in the city. A memorial statue was erected at the place of his burial. This has now been renovated and re-sited at the side of the Cathedral of St Peter and St Paul. Montgomery would have approved of the site, if not the idea of a statue. A stained glass window designed by W. F. Dixon, which is a gift from the Mappin family, adorns the east end of the sanctuary in the cathedral and is dedicated as a further memorial to James Montgomery.

This biography of James Montgomery is intended as an introduction to his life and work. For that reason it has no chapter endnotes. However, a bibliography forms an important part of the book and contains some notes for readers who wish to follow further the Montgomery story. The subtitle of the book, *A Man for all People*, was suggested by a phrase used in a lecture given by Canon Dr George Tolley, Canon Emeritus of Sheffield Cathedral, in 1999—that Montgomery was 'a man for all seasons'—and by the fact that the motto of Sheffield Cathedral is 'a place for all people'. My thanks are to them both. William Tyndale (1493–1536) was also referred to as 'a man for all seasons'; Montgomery would have approved of the association!

Acknowledgements

I t is a pleasure and a responsibility to express my thanks in the best way possible to all those who have helped to shape this biography of James Montgomery. Whatever is written here cannot really express the gratitude felt for their assistance, always enthusiastically given.

First, my thanks must go to John Wood, who has followed all the ups and downs of the script with his courteous criticisms and helpful comments. His wise advice has always been of great value and this book would not have been completed without his unfailing encouragement. Anthony Lacey has also assisted me from his experience of history and literature. I have been encouraged by my friends and colleagues on the Executive Committee of The Wesley Fellowship: Dr Herbert McGonigle, William Graham and John Gibby. My good friend Dr Peter Gentry always provided a listening ear when the going was tough.

Montgomery's association with Sheffield has brought me in touch with Gill McGregor and Dr George Tolley of the cathedral staff, and I am grateful for their help. Douglas Hindmarch of the Sheffield City Library and Carole Darlow of the Montgomery Archives have provided helpful material from their collections. I am grateful to them. In writing of Montgomery's longer poems I have been helped by Dr George Wiley's book listed in the bibliography. The book could not have been written without help from my Moravian friends: Margaret Connor at Fulneck, Edna Cooper in Northern Ireland and Lorraine Parsons at the Moravian Archives in London. Nearer home, I need to acknowledge the help from Dorothy Porter and the staff of the Leicestershire County Library in Wigston. I am grateful to my friend Derek Foreman, who for two years and more has endured my endless chatter about the subject of this book. I am glad that my friends include Phil Poncelet and Johnny Hutton, who have willingly provided the technical expertise and copying skills I do not have. Thank you.

Efforts have been made to trace the sources and possible extant copyright which might apply to the pictures in the book. If any such further consents were required and have been inadvertently overlooked, my sincere apologies are extended. Thanks are particularly due to the Moravian Church and the Sheffield City Library.

Revd Paul and Faith Cook of Derby, with their experience of books and publishing, have gently encouraged me along the way, and I am grateful to them.

My wife, Margaret, and my family have been patient and understanding. Margaret has the happy knack of seeing errors which I have missed!

My heartfelt thanks are also given to John Roberts, General Director of Day One Christian Ministries, UK, and Jim Holmes, Director of Publications, for their encouragement; to Suzanne Mitchell, editor, for her painstaking and friendly editing of the text; and to Dr Digby James, for his skilful handling of the illustrations and much more. Without them the book would not be available to the public.

My thanks to you all, and to any I might have inadvertently missed. Above all, thanks be to God for his unfailing grace.

Historical note

At points throughout the text, mention is made of various sums of money. It is worth bearing in mind that, according to the National Archives at Kew, £1 in 1840 would have a spending value today of about £45.

James Montgomery (from the *Evangelical Magazine*, March 1838)

Unfolding powers

Young though we be, and in the prime
Of life's unfolding powers,
Of all the moments of our time,
This, only this, is ours.

('Children Praising God for
His Care over Them', pub. 1867)

Family matters

The name Montgomery may be found in almost every period of British history. Certainly it appears as early as the 11th-century Domesday Book. It occurs as the name of landed gentry and Army officers as early as 1641. Revd George Montgomery was a Protestant Bishop of Clogher in 1605. Perhaps the most famous person in modern times to hold the name, Field Marshall Bernard Law Montgomery of Alamein (1887–1976), was the fourth of nine children born to Revd Henry Montgomery, a bishop on the island of Tasmania from 1889 to 1901.

James Montgomery knew little of his ancestry but believed that his name originated from Ayrshire in Scotland, the place of his birth. His great-grandfather was apparently a gentleman estate-owner.

John Montgomery, James's father, was born in January 1734 in the parish of Ahoghill in what is now Northern Ireland. He owed his Christian rebirth to the Moravian preacher and evangelist John Cennick, whose work helped to form the Moravian settlement and congregation at Gracehill near Ballymena in County Antrim. The arrival of Cennick in Ireland heralded a revival of Christ-focused living in the communities of Gloonan and Ballymena.

The Moravian settlement in Gracehill was established between 1758 and 1765 and it remains a thriving example of Moravian life and witness. John Montgomery was received into the Moravian congregation at Ballymena on 9 February 1757. Some three years later, he was sent to a similar Moravian settlement at Fulneck, now in West Yorkshire, and to a Moravian training establishment in Germany, to be prepared for the Moravian ministry. He returned to Ahoghill and Gracehill as a trained Moravian pastor and preacher.

James Montgomery's mother, Mary Blackley, the daughter of Robert Blackley, was born on 9 October 1742 and was received into the Moravian congregation at Gloonan in April 1760. Like John Montgomery, her father had been brought into the Christian faith through the preaching of John Cennick. Robert Blackley was described by James Montgomery in later years as a highly respectable member of the community; his maternal grandmother he described as 'a grave and serious matron …'

The marriage of John Montgomery and Mary Blackley took place in the parish church at Ahoghill on 27 December 1768. A good Christmas was no doubt enjoyed by all! The Gracehill records show that the newly wedded Montgomerys were among the first married couples to move into the recently established Gracehill settlement.

John and Mary had four children. Mary Ann died at the age of eighteen months in August 1771. She was the first Moravian to be buried in the new burial ground in Ayrshire. James Montgomery, whose life-story we are following, was the second child; he was followed by his two brothers, Robert and Ignatius.

Little is known of the life of Robert. He devoted himself to commerce in London. His business, mainly conducted in the Woolwich area of the capital, was that of a provision merchant. He married and had two daughters, Harriet and Elizabeth. There are occasional references to Robert in James Montgomery's *Memoirs*, and although the brothers remained in friendly contact with each other, Robert did not seem to play a significant part in James's life.

It was somewhat different with Ignatius, who followed his father into the Moravian ministry. James's youngest brother trained in Fulneck from 1783 to about 1790. He went to work in Bedford, then returned to teach at his old school in Fulneck, after which he was prepared for the Moravian ministry. He spent several years from 1804 at Gracehill. In 1808 he married Mary Agnes Steinhauer. He was appointed minister at Gracefields in the north of Ireland, serving there for two years. The family, including their first son John James, then moved to Ockbrook near Derby. After only one year, Ignatius moved to London and then to Bristol. He and his wife also had two daughters. Ill-health brought Ignatius to retirement in 1818. In the obituary written by his brother James, reference is made to a serious fall which eventually confined Ignatius to a wheelchair. For twenty years he was cared for in Ockbrook by his devoted wife until his death in April 1841 at the age of 64.

In October 1770 Revd John Montgomery was appointed to the pastoral charge of the Moravian congregation in Irvine, a small seaport in Ayrshire, Scotland. Irvine has been described as 'the only spot in Scotland where those godly men [Moravians] found a footing'. John and Mary Montgomery were therefore pioneers of the Moravian cause in Scotland, perhaps a fitting preparation for their later missionary endeavours in the West Indies.

They began their work in Irvine in March 1771, living in a small house built as part of the Moravian chapel to serve the town. Here it was that James was born and first saw the light of a Scottish day. It was indeed a modest home. The Montgomerys were recalled to Gracehill in May 1776 when James was just a child of five. James's stay in Ireland was brief, however, as in 1777 he was taken to Fulneck in Yorkshire for his education.

On 4 July 1783 John and Mary were called and commissioned to missionary work in the West Indies by the Gracehill congregation, and they left Ireland on 3 August that year. By this time, James was a youth of twelve, his brothers still only nine and seven. They were entrusted to the care of the good Moravian folk in Fulneck. The work in the West Indies was tough, often discouraging, and relatively short lived.

For six years John and Mary toiled in the cause of the gospel in Barbados. Their ministry was then moved to Tobago, where they had been occasional visitors. The hardships of life and a terrifying hurricane eventually told on Mary, and she died in the care of her husband on 23 October 1790 at the age of forty-eight. John Montgomery returned to Barbados in March 1791, but by the summer of that year ill-health had taken hold of the Moravian missionary and he died on 27 June 1791.

The death of James Montgomery's parents touched the heart of the poet. An extract from a poem written in their memory shows both his poetic gift and the warmth of affection in which he held his parents:

The cottage in Irvine, Scotland, where Montgomery was born in 1771 (Moravian Church, *The Moravian History Magazine,* James Montgomery Issue 1994)

My parents dwelt a little while
Upon a small Atlantic isle ...
Then came a hurricane,—as all
Heaven's arch, like Dagon's house, would fall,
And crush, 'midst one wild, wailing cry,
Earth in the ruins of the sky.
Beneath their humble cottage roof, ...
My father bowed his aching head
About my mother's dying bed:

From lip to lip, from heart to heart,
Passed the few parting words—'We part!'
But echoed back, though unexpressed,
'We meet again!'—rose from each breast.
Amidst the elemental strife,
That was the brightest hour of life:
Eternity outshone the tomb,
The power of God was in the room.   (unnamed fragment pub. in *Memoirs*, 1854)

The Moravians

James Montgomery said that he recollected little of his early childhood. In an interview with James Everett he said whimsically, 'I was born in Scotland and barely escaped being an Irishman. I left Scotland when I was better than four years of age and went into Ireland with my parents where I remained till I was six.' He continued, 'my recollections are those of childhood.' His memories of Irvine were chiefly scenes of nature and unusual objects which he observed in the vicinity of his home.

His parents' devotion to the Moravian cause, however, helped to shape James's character, and this was to come to full flowering in later years. James arrived at Fulneck in Yorkshire when he was six years old and he stayed until he was sixteen. It was here, among the devout evangelical people who lived in the settlement, that James could observe and in some youthful measure absorb the devotion and beliefs of the Moravian Church. It was but a fragile hold he had then on Moravian piety, one which was largely to evaporate when cast into the world of his chosen career before returning in renewed devotion. But that is a later story!

The rather better-known life of Charles Wesley can only be really appreciated with some knowledge of his home in Epworth, with its powerful parental moulding of personality and character. Charles Wesley's devotion to the Anglican Church of his parents never wavered during his life, even though the remarkable events of Whitsuntide 1738 brought a new personal faith in Christ with an assurance of God's saving grace. All this made Wesley the man and the Christian that he was. Similarly, the formative years among the Brethren at Fulneck and the

Fulneck Moravian settlement, Pudsey (founded 1746, opened 1748)

memory of his parents' devotion to Christ helped to make Montgomery the man that he became.

The Moravian Church has an ancient history. Its origins belong to the early years of the 15th century, when followers of the Christian martyr John Huss suffered violent and relentless persecution in their homelands of Bohemia and Moravia. The small 'hidden seed' of Christians survived several attempts to destroy them and their witness during the period of the Counter-Reformation. In the early 18th century (1722), a group of them found their way to the settlements of Count Nikolaus von Zinzendorf, a Lutheran nobleman in Saxony. There, in 1727, the 'Unitas Fratrum', as they had become known, experienced an extraordinary work of God's Holy Spirit which gave them an impetus for worldwide evangelism. The Moravians were thus a pioneer church, and remain so today.

The pioneering spirit of the Moravians took many of them out of the somewhat comfortable life of the Zinzendorf settlement at Herrnhut and, with the support and encouragement of the godly Count, into the unknown world with the gospel of saving grace and faith. Their missionary and pioneer endeavours took them to the West Indies, Greenland, Labrador in Canada, South Africa, America and England. In England the Moravians established themselves in London and had such a powerful influence on the 18th-century revival as they came into vital contact with leaders such as George Whitefield and John Wesley. It may well have been this pioneering spirit which gave James Montgomery his enthusiastic vision of world evangelism which was such an important feature in his later life.

The Moravians are, of course, a Protestant church following the doctrines of Luther and the Reformers who followed him. The Moravians largely endorse the doctrines of the Augsburg Confession of 1530, which was drafted by Martin Luther and three colleagues and which enshrine the tenets of the Protestant evangelical faith. The basic Moravian doctrines can therefore be summarized as:

- Original sin affects all people and brings eternal death to all who are not reborn by the Holy Spirit.
- We cannot be justified by our own strength, merits or works, but only on account of Christ through faith.

- The church will remain for ever. It is the congregation of the saints through which the gospel is rightly proclaimed and the sacraments rightly administered.
- The human will has some liberty in the accomplishment of civil righteousness, but without the Holy Spirit it has no power to accomplish the righteousness of God or spiritual righteousness.
- Works cannot reconcile man to God or merit remission of sins—salvation is only by faith in Christ.
- It is necessary, however, to do good works, not in order to merit grace, but because it is the will of God.

In the body of Moravian doctrine there is a very powerful emphasis on the atonement through the cross—the shedding of the blood of the Lamb—and in the 17th–18th centuries this doctrine generally cast its light over all others. These doctrines formed the solid foundations of James Montgomery's personal confession and found their way into his witness and work, especially his hymns.

The Moravian Church is a liturgical church, which perhaps explains the friendly links between it and the Church of England which have been maintained for three centuries and were enjoyed by James Montgomery. The Moravian Church had 18th-century links with Methodism and shares the Wesleyan emphases of salvation by faith alone and the call to a holy life. Again, Montgomery, in all his years in Sheffield, enjoyed fellowship with the people called Methodists.

It is customary in Moravian congregations for infants to be baptized, usually by sprinkling. This has not adversely affected their association with the historic Baptist churches, and gave them a point of contact with independent churches. Montgomery, while adopting the Moravian faith and being persuaded as to the truth of his Protestant evangelical doctrines, could practise friendly engagement with others who held different views on matters he regarded as non-essential. He was a man for all people, yet distinctly his own man.

Moravian congregations gave joyful expression to their faith in the singing of psalms, hymns and spiritual songs. Members of the Zinzendorf congregations in Saxony sang the hymns of the great German writers Martin Luther, Paul Gerhardt and Gerhard Tersteegen, as well, of course, as Zinzendorf's own contribution to the rich variety of hymns of the 17th and 18th centuries. It was the Moravian love of singing, even in adversity, that captured the heart of John Wesley on his journey to Georgia in 1735. He quickly learned the German language in order to sing with his new friends and then translate some thirty hymns into the English language so that, in the fullness of the coming revival, Moravian hymns and those of his brother Charles would edify and confirm the faith of so many new converts. It is little wonder that James Montgomery, steeped as he was in the music and hymns of the Fulneck Christians, and with the gifts with which he was endowed, became a foremost hymn-writer.

Fulneck

James Montgomery began his formal education at the Fulneck Moravian School on 16 October 1777. He later observed that this was the day when his English life commenced; years later, it was on this same day that he was imprisoned in York Castle for seditious libel.

John Montgomery and his young son had travelled from Gracehill, embarking at Liverpool and making their way to Fulneck, the place chosen by James's parents for his formal education. Of the voyage to England, Montgomery late wrote, 'We had a terrible storm. I was, as might be expected, much afraid, but my father told me to trust in the Lord Jesus who had saved the Apostles on the water. I did so and felt composed.' Later, James wrote that he was told that '… such was the danger to which they had been exposed that the captain himself was violently agitated and pointing to me who sate [sic] composed and resigned, he said, "I would give a thousand pounds for the faith of that child."'

The Moravian folk who helped to found the settlement at Fulneck expressed their faith and vision in this statement of intent:

The aim in erecting this village was, that we might dwell together in true unity of the faith, in brotherly love and simplicity of heart under the direction of the only head of the church, our Lord Jesus Christ, and the gracious leading of the Holy Spirit, agreeable to the last will of our Lord, John xvii, and that we might under the protection of our most gracious sovereign, lead a quiet and peaceable life in all Godliness and honesty.

In 1735, the first Moravian brethren to come to England were on their
way to America with the message of salvation by faith in Jesus Christ when
they providentially met John and Charles Wesley and their companion,
Benjamin Ingham, on the *Simmons* as they too took to the high seas on
their way to Georgia with a similar purpose. It was James Hutton, a friend
of both the Wesleys and the Moravians, who was instrumental in founding
a small but influential society in Fetter Lane, London, which in 1742
became the first Moravian congregation in England.

Benjamin Ingham soon returned from Georgia and found his way to

Moravian settlement, Pudsey (from Holland and Everett, *Memoirs of James Montgomery,* vol. 2,
1855, p. 82)

Yorkshire. He set to work to evangelize in the county of the broad acres and within a few years he had founded over forty societies. The Moravians identified with Ingham's evangelistic endeavours, and eventually the Inghamite societies were handed over to Moravian supervision.

Count Zinzendorf visited Yorkshire for the first time in 1743 and chose the site where the Fulneck settlement was to be built on the model of Herrnhut. The Moravian policy was, as far as practicable, to find high ground for their village communities. Benjamin Ingham purchased the property at Fulneck which the Count had identified. The first foundations were laid in 1746, only two years after the purchase of the site. Fulneck became 'a city set on a hill'; in typical Moravian fashion it was also known as 'Lambshill'. Within the space of a few years, the Moravian settlement was well established.

Although the Moravian communal policy is not monastic there were separate dwellings for male and female residents and a segregated system for the education of girls and boys. Despite this degree of formal segregation, residents were also a family and a worshipping community and congregation. The rules at the time of Montgomery's stay at Fulneck were seriously, if also kindly, imposed.

The 'House Orders', or rules for residential life, stated that the Brethren must live together in brotherly love and harmony. Presumably the same applied to sisters! Brethren were not be in bed after 6 a.m. in the summer and 7 a.m. in the winter, nor were they to stay out of bed after 11 p.m. Meals, it was decreed, were to be 'seemly'. Children had to abstain from reading 'hurtful' or 'unprofitable' books and 'take care' in their conversations.

Policies which further governed the Brethren, 'Brothers' Agreements', as they were known, stressed the importance of education, and great emphasis was to be paid to the manner of early training.

The children's boarding schools, or 'Children's Oeconomies', as they were known, were established in about 1741, several years before they were transferred to Fulneck. Originally, we are told, they were more like orphanages than schools, but they did eventually change their character until, by the time of Montgomery a few decades later, they were even opened to non-Moravian pupils. Parents were requested to sign an agreement not to take their children away without consent. The declaration contained the following words: 'Being earnestly desirous to have my children preserved from the seductions of this world and brought up for Him who has shed His blood for them ...'

The 'School Curriculum' for 1761, not materially different from that which Montgomery would encounter a couple of decades later, required that pupils would begin the day at 7:30 a.m. with musical exercises, often on the harpsichord, copy accounting, and spinning and winding—for boys! The later part of the morning would be occupied with writing, or 'ciphering'. Afternoon classes included Scripture or Bible history, reading and spelling. Oral and written examinations were held regularly for all the subjects taught in the Oeconomies.

It is possible to glean from the *Memoirs* of James Montgomery some idea of what school at Fulneck was like for the budding writer. Montgomery clearly regarded his arrival, residence and training at the Fulneck settlement as part of God's plan for his life and work. He expresses this conviction in the words of a poem written in later life and entitled 'Departed Days':

For hither from my native climb,
The hand that leads Orion forth
And leads Arcturus round the north,
Brought me in life's exulting prime.
Blest be that hand! Whether it shed
Mercies or judgement on my head:
Extend the sceptre or exalt the rod,
Blest be that hand! It is the hand of God.   ('Departed Days: A Rhapsody', 1806)

Early in his education James was introduced by his English teacher, Job Bradley, to *The Pilgrim's Progress* and *Robinson Crusoe*. It was his parents' strong desire that he should be trained for the Moravian ministry, as his father had been, and his studies were designed to that end. Consequently, James was introduced to the Latin, Greek, German and French languages. Montgomery records that, 'The master took several children out one day and read to them, behind the hedge, Blair's *The*

Grave', and then he goes on to describe the effect on him. He writes, 'my attention was strongly arrested, and a few lines made a powerful impression on my mind; I said to myself, "If ever I become a poet, I will write something like this."' He then explained that later, when he became a man, he would write a 'round' poem, because the idea of 'round' to him meant perfection. A round globe was perfect and anything added to it might augment its size but could never add to its perfection! He went on to observe that his intention to compose a 'round' poem was his beau idéal. Here, then, lie the origins of Montgomery's constant aim for perfection in all his life's work.

The School Curriculum, which determined not only the subject matter but also the teaching and learning methods, introduced the young boy to the subjects of general history, geography and music. Indeed, English and music, he tells us, were his chief delights. Montgomery's schooldays were not, however, marked by a passionate devotion to learning. His youthful and active mind was sometimes affected by periods of illness. Other boys were also careless about reading, and James wrote in 1794,

even when I was driven like a coal ass through the Latin and Greek grammars, I was distinguished for nothing but indolence and melancholy, brought upon me by a raging and lingering fever with which I was suddenly seized one fine summer day as I lay under a hedge with my companions, listening to our master whilst he read some animated passages from Blair's poem ... *The Grave*. My happier school-fellows, born under milder planets, all fell asleep ... but I, who am always asleep when I ought to be waking, never dreamed of closing an eye but eagerly caught the contagious malady; and from that ecstatic moment to the present, Heaven knows, I have never known one cheerful, peaceful night.

Even allowing perhaps some degree of retrospective exaggeration, it is not difficult to see the germs of some of Montgomery's mental enthusiasm for what he liked and indifference towards what did not take his fancy. It may serve as a salutary reminder to parents that children, even so young, find their charted course somewhat easier if they are given gentle encouragements.

Because the education policy at Fulneck was to scrutinize all reading material and to control carefully the reading of unauthorized books, the young James was somewhat limited in what he could legitimately read. Even so, at about ten years of age he could write, 'I was as much a master of Homer and Virgil as Pope or Dryden's translations could make me.' Before the age of ten he was discouraged from reading the eminent English poets, but he relates that a schoolfriend received from his father a collection of works by Milton, Thomson and Young. The book was carefully examined by one of the masters and all unsuitable passages were unceremoniously torn from the treasured gift. Montgomery says that the book was handed back in a mangled state and his friend was mortified.

Later, when he was in Sheffield, he recalled the story of a young lad, whom he described as being no taller than a shop counter, asking if he could obtain from James a sixpenny copy of *Jane Shore*, an 'adult' book about the mistress of King Edward IV; Montgomery replied, 'You, little fellow, why do you want to read that book ...? Go instantly!' After the boy had made a hasty exit Montgomery reflected to a companion, 'Who knows but that is a young Roscius [a handsome and very famous actor in the Ancient Roman Empire]? One of the first things that gave me a desire to read ... was an extract from Hamlet ... which I read at school ... but we were prohibited from reading the whole play, but that very prohibition ... created in me the most ardent desire to see the whole ...'

Commenting again on his rather isolated life at school, Montgomery recalls somewhat resentfully, 'During the whole of this long period [ten years], I was carefully secluded ... from my commerce with the world, as if I had been imprisoned in a cloister. I do not recall having once ... conversed for ten minutes with any person whatever, except my companions, our master or occasional Moravian visitors.' The motive for this confined life, he says, was to maintain and influence piety; he comments, 'Whatever we did was done for the sake and in the name of Jesus Christ ... whom we were taught to regard in the amiable and endearing light of a friend and brother.'

Montgomery continues with this insight into the significance and effect of the Moravian discipline and piety: 'There is no system of religion which I have yet seen, which, taking it all in all, has half the charms for a young, a warm, a feeling heart as that professed by these people'; he continues with his memories of earlier times: 'I once believed, I once enjoyed its blessings, I once was happy.' He tells us that he had been troubled from infancy by his temperament. He was clearly writing in such a way during a troubled time. Happily, as we shall see, he largely conquered his tendency towards sadness and despondency, becoming, as he describes it, 'happy again'.

Despite the trying restrictions imposed by the Moravian regime at Fulneck, James tells us that he frequently found ways to borrow books and stealthily imbibe as much knowledge as he could. 'All mankind are [*sic*] made much in the same mould, curiosity and an enquiring mind cannot be artificially subdued for ever.' Of religion, he says it was eventually brought before the court of enquiry in his own heart: he studied, he reasoned, he doubted, and he almost disbelieved. To explain, he goes on, 'I hitherto adhered to the credit of my tutors; simplicity once lost can never be retained.' It was the lifelong regret of the poet that he did once lose his simple faith.

One aspect of life at Fulneck which frequently filled him with joy and helped him through his difficult times was the joyful singing of hymns. The hymns, and the way in which they were sung, made an indelible impression on his youthful mind and heart. He recalls that he produced a small collection of his own hymns and poems when he was a teenage pupil.

On a somewhat lighter note, here is Montgomery telling the tale of a mealtime curiosity. It was the custom for boys of different classes to occasionally take meals together. James was in the ninth year and was placed with boys of his own age. That day the beverage was changed. All the boys formed a circle and sang a hymn, and one boy was nominated to say a prayer. He knelt and prayed, 'Lord, bless us little children, and make us very good. We thank thee for this food. Bless this good chocolate to us, and give us more of it!' 'We all thought it was the expression of our hearts,' commented James.

Occasionally, the somewhat mundane life at Fulneck was enlivened by important visitors. Montgomery tells us that he did not remember the visit of John Wesley, but, according to Wesley's Journal, he did pay the Moravians a visit in April 1780, when he was shown around the whole establishment except the schools. That Montgomery did not recall this visit by the Methodist leader is perhaps not too surprising in view of the unfortunate tension between the Moravians and John Wesley in earlier years and the fact that Wesley was not introduced to the schoolchildren in their classes. It is a credit to Montgomery that the uneasiness which he may have felt on the matter of the Moravian-Wesleyan relationship did not sour his later life, when he found the Methodists helpful to him in Sheffield and supportive of his work in the city. As a man who thrived on friendship with many different groups of people, it was fortunate that in the absence of any Moravian witness in Sheffield, Montgomery was warmly embraced by the Methodists.

Another famous visitor to the 'city set on a hill' was the Moravian bishop Johannes de Watteville, who was also the son-in-law of Count Zinzendorf, having married the Count's eldest daughter, Henrietta Benigna Justina. 'Brother Johannes' addressed the boys, and 'Sister Benigna' spoke to the girls. After this we are told that the good bishop, whom Montgomery described as a large and most venerable man with a lofty curled wig, kissed the boys on both cheeks and his wife saluted the girls; all the boys, however, kissed her hand.

Before James left school, he began to familiarize himself with the English hymn-writers. In his later schooldays he was also able to read the works of the noble poets (Burns, Byron, Shelley and Wordsworth, for example). He tells us that, at about the age of sixteen, he became familiar with the works of Cowper of Olney. His high view of Cowper's work did not prevent him from a somewhat exalted and uncharacteristic opinion that 'I thought I could write better verses myself'. Even before leaving school, his fondness for and devotion to the writing of poetry led him to frequent retirement to bed with a theme on his mind which he resolved to commit to writing before he went to sleep. He says, 'this habit of wakefulness … never wholly forsook me.'

Despite the earnest attention paid by Montgomery to those parts of the curriculum which attracted his interest—music and writing—the school authorities were not entirely happy with his efforts. Here is a paraphrase of how the compilers of the Montgomery *Memoirs* described the end of James's schooldays: With regret the Moravians witnessed the growing tendency of Montgomery to silent and unaccountable distraction, which, in their opinion, rendered their pupil incurable. Entries in the school diary for 4 March 1786 show that, presumably as an incentive, Montgomery was to remain in the school to be trained as a master; when this was told to him, he seemed pleased. However, a diary entry for 2 May 1787 noted that he was not using his proper diligence in his studies and he was admonished. One month later, despite repeated warnings, there was apparently no improvement and it was decided to put him into business. It is a fact that Montgomery used some rather strong language to record his displeasure; he said he was turned out of the school at Fulneck on account of indolence.

It is quite strange that, according to the editors of the Montgomery *Memoirs*, the master so influential in Montgomery's decline at Fulneck was none other than a German teacher with the name of Molther, the son of the preacher associated with the Wesleys. Molther had a role at Fulneck as a musician, and it was he who gave Montgomery tuition in playing the harpsichord, as well as striking him with his fiddlestick! James had a lowly opinion of the junior Molther. James Montgomery left Fulneck, and so ended his interesting but sometimes turbulent training at 'the city set on a hill'. This also marked the beginning of a period of unsettled wanderings in the south of Yorkshire, the White Rose County.

The wanderer

At fond sixteen my roving heart
Was pierced by love's delightful dart;
Keen transport throbbed through every vein,—
I never felt so sweet a pain!   ('Hannah', 1801)

Mirfield

The godly Moravians at Fulneck, though distressed by their talented but difficult pupil, were nevertheless unwilling to release him into an inhospitable world. They arranged for James to be taken into the care of a Moravian businessman in the town of Mirfield, ten miles south of Fulneck and adjacent to the larger town of Huddersfield. The desire of the Fulneck Moravians to encourage Montgomery to take seriously his parents' wishes concerning training for the ministry was seemingly at an end. By placing him in Mirfield they hoped to divert him from the day-dreams of fame which captivated the mind and heart of the still impressionable youth.

The businessman of Mirfield was a devout Moravian who had a successful retail bakery business. His name was Lockwood. For Montgomery, this move meant that he was no longer committed to serious structured study and was therefore unlikely to fulfil his parents' wishes. That being so, it is fair to say that in later years Montgomery never ceased to have some regrets that he determined his own course of life. Of his departure from the 'religious orbit' of Fulneck he wrote in retrospect,

A star from heaven went astray
A planet beautiful and bright;
Which to the sun's diviner ray
Owed all its beauty and its light ...
A secret impulse urged its course,
As by a demon-power possest,
With rash, unheeding, headlong force,
It wildly wandered seeking rest ...

At length amidst the abyss of space,
Beyond attraction's marvellous spell,
It lost the sense of time and place,
And thought itself invisible:
Though suns and systems rolled afar,
Without companions went that star.

(unnamed fragment pub. in *Memoirs*)

So James Montgomery came to Mirfield in 1788 as a gifted but undisciplined youth. Little is known of his work at the bakery under the kindly Lockwood's supervision, but apparently he had little to do with serving customers or learning about either bakery or accountancy. Rather, he was occupied with composing poetry. His poem 'Alfred' was written at Mirfield, as were several other minor works. A poetic version of Psalm 113 was penned; his love for the Bible was not altogether extinguished.

At Fulneck, Montgomery's talent and fondness for music-making had developed. The Moravians, a music-loving people, encouraged him to express his musical gifts by providing tuition in various instruments. Next to composing poetry, James's favourite occupation was to make and hear music. As he put it himself, in the little retail shop of the 'fine bread baker' at Mirfield he used to 'misspend his time' in the composition of music. He said that he was 'music mad' and he used to 'blow his brains out' on the hautboy (oboe). His love of poetry and music in combination was eventually to blossom into the gifted hymn-writing on which his fame was mainly to rest.

The Moravian baker regularly attended the 'preaching of the Brethren' in Mirfield, but it was only infrequently that James Montgomery attended with him. Indeed, on the Sunday morning of 19 June 1789, having packed a few of his belongings, which included his poetry, he slipped quietly away from Mirfield and found himself on the highway and heading southwards to an entirely unknown destination.

This is how Montgomery reflects on his time at the Lockwood bakery:

Here, at Mirfield, having little to do but amuse myself, I grew more unhappy and discontented ... in an evil hour, I determined to break loose and see the world. I was not bound [by apprenticeship] to my master, and knew that if I left him, the Moravians would not compel me to return ... though I was only sixteen years old [he was, in fact, eighteen].

He continues, in a mildly humorous way, to tell us that his worldly goods consisted of the clothes on his back, a single change of linen, and three and sixpence (17.5 pence today!) in his pocket. He concludes, 'I therefore left him [Lockwood] and ... at the age of eighteen set out to begin to see the world!' Now 'free' he certainly was, and perhaps for the first time in his life he felt as though he had broken the firm but gentle hold of his Moravian influences. The authors of Montgomery's *Memoirs* reflect that he sometimes looked behind him in a pensive and even regretful mood and harboured thoughts of returning to the familiar 'home' where he had been shown such kindness.

Montgomery left Mirfield just as Abraham left Ur, 'not knowing where he was going' (see Heb. 11:8). By instinct, but perhaps to travel in the opposite direction from Fulneck, he headed southwards into the unknown and unfamiliar world of what is now South Yorkshire.

Wentworth

Montgomery might soon have arrived in Sheffield, the city he made his home in later years. On reaching Wakefield, however, he stopped to consider which way he should turn. The road on which he was travelling had a turning to the south-east and to the south-west. After some deliberation, and surely by God's directing hand, he took the road towards Rotherham. Where he lodged overnight is unknown, but eventually turning south, he arrived in Wentworth, a small village dominated by the palatial residence and grounds of the fifth Earl Fitzwilliam (1786–1857).

The Fitzwilliams had taken residence at Wentworth House in 1782 and by the mid-nineteenth century they were among the richest families in England. It was towards evening when the young Montgomery arrived in Wentworth and found hospitality in a small public house in the humble hamlet. On this, his first of several visits to Wentworth, Montgomery was not to know that the grand house of Earl Fitzwilliam would be the place which he would later visit as an honoured guest.

It was during his brief stay that Montgomery met another young man, Joshua Hunt, who had come to Wentworth on an errand for his father. The Hunts were family grocers in the nearby village of Wath-on-Dearne. Holland and Everett record for us that, seeing a strange youth in the room with a small travelling bundle beside him and apparently a little uncomfortable, the junior Hunt made a tentative approach to James to offer some companionship. During the conversation Hunt mentioned that his father had a grocery business and was looking for an assistant to work in his shop. Montgomery decided that this might be a possible step to take and made an application for the position in Wath-on-Dearne. Joshua Hunt's father was a cautious man and he agreed to employ Montgomery only if he could obtain the consent of his previous master and Moravian guardian at Mirfield. Montgomery therefore apparently returned to Wentworth to await a reply from Mirfield. Meanwhile, as Hunt asserts, it was during Montgomery's anxious time of waiting in Wentworth that he had an extraordinary meeting with Earl Fitzwilliam.

Montgomery had probably heard of the Earl's friendly disposition. Moreover, he knew that the great man was at home because he could see him riding in his grounds. So the young poet apparently took one of his compositions to present to the Earl in person. He entered the parklands of the country house, where he met the Earl and handed him a copy of his poem. With characteristic friendliness, the Earl read it there and then, and James was handed a 'golden guinea' for his efforts. This was the first payment James was to receive for his poetic work. It should be said that the detailed evidence for this Fitzwilliam–Montgomery encounter is not as firm as we would like it to be, but there can be no doubt that some incident such as this did occur.

During his short stay in Wentworth, Montgomery was not idle. He appears to have paid a visit to Masborough on the outskirts of Rotherham to witness the casting, boring and turning of heavy-metal ornaments. He was also able to see the parts being forged for an iron bridge to be set up experimentally in London under the supervision of Thomas Paine. Meanwhile, he awaited the news from Mirfield and Fulneck which he hoped would give consent for his work in the Hunt establishment in Wath-on-Dearne. Here is Montgomery's own version of his appeal to his guardian, reproduced as an example of his literary style:

When I had been on my travels about four days, I then wrote as I had always intended to do, to my master; indeed I left a letter behind me, declaring in plain terms, the uneasiness of my mind, and saying that he should hear from me. I wrote to him to require a character, or commendation to a situation which I had heard of; conscious that no moral guilt could be laid to my charge, and that in all my dealings I had served him with the strictest integrity. My master laid my letter before the council of Moravian ministers, who meet at Fulneck to regulate the affairs of their society; and they unanimously agreed to write any recommendation for me which I might require, if I obstinately persisted in my resolution to leave them; but instructed him to make me any offers, and if possible, to bring me back again. He came to me in person, at Rotherham, where I waited for an answer. I was so affected by his appearance, that I ran to meet him in the inn-yard; and he was so overwhelmed with the tenderness at the sight of me, that we clasped each other's arms as he sat on horseback, and remained weeping without speaking a word, for some time, to the great amusement of the very many spectators. The spectators may have been amused with the sight; but we think the reader will be affected by such an evidence of mutual esteem between parties so circumstanced. It required all my resolution to resist his entreaties and persuasion to return; but I at length overcame; and when he left me next day, he gave a very handsome written character, and also called himself on my future employer to recommend me to him. He also supplied me with money, and sent me clothes and other things which I had left behind.

The way was now clear for James to travel to Wath to take the next important step in the journey of life.

Wath-on-Dearne

James Montgomery took up his position in Wath-on-Dearne at the age of eighteen. The Hunt family business was described as a 'general store' and was situated in the centre of the village. Wath-on-Dearne was often referred to by its inhabitants as 'the queen of villages'. Its name in the Domesday records is 'Wade'. The village is situated in what was then pleasant low-lying land adjacent to the Dearne and Dove canal and on the banks of the river Dearne. It is located three miles from Wentworth. In the time of the Hunts it had several other shops and the population was employed mainly in the coal mines and iron workshops which provided the prosperity of the village folk.

Montgomery soon settled into his work and his new life with the family who had employed him. Holland and Everett comment that 'he was remarkably grave, nervous and silent, exemplary, steady and industrious … ' He intensified his interest in composing poetry and playing music. In nearby Swinton village James found a like-minded friend in a Mr Bramhall who kept a stationer's shop. Bramhall was an encourager, a Barnabas-type

The house in which Montgomery lived in Wath-on-Dearne (from Holland and Everett, *Memoirs of James Montgomery,* vol. 1, 1854, p. 87)

man, and both benefited from the friendship. Apart from visits to Swinton and occasional contact with the Moravians, Montgomery seems to have spent most of his leisure hours with his new employers, and he became warmly attached to them. It is of some interest that, although he had largely broken free from his early Moravian influences, he had not entirely forsaken his spiritual heritage. On one occasion he had the opportunity to write a prayer for the use of Mrs Hunt, who was 'labouring under the severe affliction'. The prayer, preserved in Montgomery's handwriting and which is too long to reproduce here in full, contains phrases characteristic of the Moravian emphasis on the suffering love of Christ the Saviour. Some expressions used in the prayer indicate its intense spirituality:

Above all we adore Thy undeserved love in giving up Thy only son ... to be a sacrifice for us!

Justice and mercy kissed each other, the flaming sword of justice was quickened in our heart by the blood of the redeemer and mercy opened the gates of paradise to us ...

May none of those whom Thou O Father hast given him be lost and eternity itself shall be too short to sing Thy praise.

Two things stand out from this prayer. Firstly, it gives a remarkable insight into the mind and heart of an eighteen-year-old who had apparently turned his back on the Moravian way of life for a life in the world. Secondly, there are no words of petition for the healing of the suffering or comfort for the lady for whom it was penned!

After Montgomery had been in the Hunt employment for about a year, he took the decision to travel to London. His plan to visit the capital city was preceded by his sending a volume of his poetry, accompanied by a letter from his friend Bramhall, to the bookseller Harrison in Paternoster Row. Montgomery followed his collection of poems to see what London had to offer. The comparatively quiet life beside the river Dearne was exchanged for a different life by the river Thames. The bookseller Harrison was an active and well-known publisher. He read the collection of poems and offered the author a position in his shop. Harrison's encouragement for Montgomery to continue and develop his talent proved to be a significant influence in the life of the young poet.

Although the Paternoster shop was busy and flourishing in a city even then bustling with life, Montgomery retained his preference for the solitude and seclusion of his days in Wath. He was never interested in the worldly life or entertainment available in London. The theatres apparently held no attraction for him. He never even visited the British Museum, although on a return visit to London in 1795 he did go to Covent Garden. For a literary man this may seem surprising, but perhaps the residue of the holiness of Fulneck deterred him.

He was described at this time by an elderly acquaintance in Wath as a slender youth shrinking from the cold and still more from contact with other people. The residents of Wath regarded him as being 'no vulgar boy'. Possibly the worldliness of the capital city proved uncomfortable to the sensitive youth, or, more probably, he found fewer outlets for his poetic and musical gifts than he had expected. After an unfortunate misunderstanding with Harrison, the sadly disappointed youth determined to take his leave of London after a lonely ramble along the banks of the Thames. There and then he made up his mind to return to the less exciting but more hospitable Yorkshire. Here is Montgomery's poetic farewell to London, the city of unfulfilled dreams. The date was March 1791.

An hour may come, so I delight to dream,
When slowly wandering by the stream,
Majestic Thames! I leave the world behind,
And give to Fancy all th' enraptured mind:
An hour may come, when I shall strike the lyre
To nobler themes.

(Gifford's Mæviad)

As he travelled back to Yorkshire he was accompanied in what the authors of his *Memoirs* called the 'heavy coach' by three very different people. The commercial traveller provided no fascination for Montgomery; likewise the young woman travelling alone. The silent, serious gentleman, however, aroused his interest. Montgomery reflected, 'it would be unwise to offend him.' The name of this gentleman proved to be Captain Byron, as discovered by Montgomery from the label on his trunk! Captain Byron was the father of the celebrated poet Lord Byron. I mention this piece of apparent trivia here because it is one of the first real evidences of Montgomery's slowly developing fascination with people, their personalities and characters; a feature to be further developed in later life and marking him as a man who would eventually work so influentially in the lives of others.

So Montgomery returned to Yorkshire a 'sadder and wiser man'. To reach London as a place was easier than to reach its anticipated honour through prose, rhyme or music. His friends in Wath-on-Dearne received him back in their midst with charm, generosity and kindness. The grocer gave him back his job and he was welcomed again into the household and family circle.

Montgomery's second residence in Wath-on-Dearne was, however, to be short lived. It was part of his duty to deliver goods and collect monies at different places in the area. He visited the neighbouring villages of Great Houghton, Little Houghton and Thurnscoe, finding the journeys pleasant but the work of collecting monies less so. But the day which was to be an important turning-point in his life was not far away. Soon he would find his life's work and witness in the city of Sheffield.

It has already been mentioned that Montgomery was not a natural romantic, but he was not entirely free from the lure of love. As Dr George Tolley said in his 1999 lecture, 'Montgomery rarely explores romantic love.' There are several exceptions, the outstanding one being his poem 'Hannah', published on 29 August 1801. Dr Tolley tells us that there was a Hannah Turner who lived in Wath-on-Dearne during Montgomery's stay in the village. The Montgomery *Memoirs* fill out this connection with Hannah. Village tradition identifies her as the daughter of the Turners of Swathe Hall, situated between Wath-on-Dearne and Barnsley, which Montgomery occasionally visited. However, he hardly ever referred to Hannah Turner, and his brother Ignatius said, 'I have sounded out my brother about Hannah yet I never could learn anything more than the verses themselves [referring to the poem which follows].' Other people who knew the poet were no more successful.

Hannah Turner was married at Wath-on-Dearne on 26 May 1801 to William Mansell, a gamekeeper attached to Belvoir Castle. Soon after Mansell's death in 1811, Hannah gave birth to a child, but sadly she died a few days after giving the world her son. Through contact with James Holland some years later, Montgomery assented to the general correctness of the details related here. This chapter opened with a quotation from 'Hannah', and here is the full poem. It speaks beautifully for itself, its author and Hannah (Montgomery describes himself in the first verse as being sixteen when he met her, even though he was eighteen when he arrived in Wath-on-Dearne).

1 At fond sixteen my roving heart
Was pierced by Love's delightful dart:
Keen transport throbb'd through every vein,
—I never felt so sweet a pain!

2 Where circling woods embower'd the glade,
I met the dear romantic maid:
I stole her hand,—it shrunk,—but no;
I would not let my captive go.

3 With all the fervency of youth,
While passion told the tale of truth,
I mark'd my Hannah's downcast eye—
'Twas kind, but beautifully shy:

4 Not with a warmer, purer ray,
The Sun, enamour'd, woos young May;
Nor May, with softer maiden grace,
Turns from the Sun her blushing face.

5 But, swifter than the frighted dove,
Fled the gay morning of my love;
Ah! that so bright a morn, so soon,
Should vanish in so dark a noon.

6 The angel of Affliction rose,
And in his grasp a thousand woes;
He pour'd his vial on my head,
And all the heaven of rapture fled.

7 Yet, in the glory of my pride,
I stood,—and all his wrath defied;
I stood,—tough whirlwinds shook my brain,
And lightnings cleft my soul in twain.

8 I shunn'd my nymph—and knew not why
I durst not meet her gentle eye;
I shunn'd her,—for I could not bear
To marry her to my despair.

9 Yet, sick at heart with hope delay'd,
Oft the dear image of that maid
Glanced, like the rainbow, o'er my mind,
And promised happiness behind.

10 The storm blew o'er, and in my breast
The halcyon Peace rebuilt her nest:
The storm blew o'er, and clear and mild
The sea of Youth and Pleasure smiled.

11 'Twas on the merry morn of May,
To Hannah's cot I took my way:
My eager hopes were on the wing,
Like swallows sporting in the Spring.

12 Then, as I climb'd the mountains o'er,
I lived my wooing days once more;
And fancy sketched my married lot,
My wife, my children, and my cot.

Chapter 2

13 I saw the village steeple rise,—
My soul sprang, sparkling, in my eyes:
The rural bells rang sweet and clear,—
My fond heart listen'd in mine ear.

14 I reach'd the hamlet:—all was gay;
I love a rustic holy day;
I met a wedding,—stepp'd aside;
It pass'd,—my Hannah was the bride.

15 —There is a grief that cannot feel;
It leaves a wound that will not heal;
—My heart grew cold,—it felt not then:
When shall it cease to feel again?

(1801)

Tanya Schmoller, in her valuable collection of Montgomery's *Letters from a Newspaperman in Prison* (see Bibliography), reproduces part of a letter written by Montgomery from Scarborough in connection with this poem and dated 23 July 1796. He writes, 'In gloomy humour I wrote the preceding trifle a few days ago. You will learn from it a secret I have hitherto witheld [sic] from you and all my friends in Sheffield, namely that "I am married".' Schmoller comments in an endnote that there is no record in any biographical memoir or note that Montgomery was ever married, nor do parish registers or his will reveal anything. As an old man he alluded to his celibacy in the words, 'the secret is within myself and it is in the way to the grave from which no secret will be betrayed until the Day of Judgement'. Schmoller continues, 'A search through *The Iris* [the newspaper Montgomery later edited and in which he published 'Hannah'] of the time reveals no piece printed on the matter of his "marriage".'

It is fascinating to speculate that the 'secret within [him]self' might have been that he had 'married' his Hannah in an emotional attachment which was to him a marriage of the heart. More than a secret emotional attachment, however, there surely never was.

The Register and The Iris

1 I left the God of truth and light;
I left the God who gave me breath,
To wander in the wilds of night,
And perish in the snares of death.

2 Lo! Through the gloom of guilty tears,
My faith discerns a dawn of grace;
The sun of righteousness appears
In Jesus' reconciling face.

('The Sinner Reviewing his Ways', pub. 1867)

God, who at various times and in various ways spoke in time past to the fathers by the prophets, has in these last days spoken to us by His Son … Therefore we must give the more earnest heed to the things we have heard, lest we drift away.(Hebrews 1:1–2; 2:1)

Appointment to *The Register*

In 1825 James Montgomery was looking back on his introduction to the city of Sheffield. He wrote, 'I came to this town in the spring of 1792, a stranger and friendless, without any intention of a long residence.' His residence lasted sixty-two years!

Dr George Tolley, in his 1999 lecture, reminded his audience that Sheffield now has a Montgomery Road, Montgomery Avenue, Montgomery Drive, Montgomery Mount, Montgomery Hall and Montgomery Theatre, all fitting tributes to the man who became so much a part of his adopted city. He goes on, 'In Montgomery's day nothing of significance happened in public life without his participation and involvement.'

Montgomery's life in Sheffield began with the apparent chance sighting of an advertisement. He was out and about on his master Hunt's business of collecting money in the village of Great Houghton when he saw a copy of the Sheffield weekly newspaper *The Register*, which carried an advertisement for a position under the editor, Joseph Gales. The advertisement read,

WANTED, in a counting-house in Sheffield, A CLERK. None need apply but such as have been used to book-keeping and can produce desirable testimonials of character. Terms and specimens of writing to be left with the printer.

(Sheffield *Register*, 2 March 1792)

Montgomery applied for the post. After an interview with the editor, his application was successful and he took up his new position in April 1792. At first the post was for a probationary period, but soon his new master Gales was satisfied and Montgomery became a permanent and respected member on the staff of the newspaper.

Montgomery reflects on his arrival in the city: 'I came … to Sheffield. I had fondly, foolishly sacrificed all my friends, connections and prospects … and thrown myself headlong into the world.'

It was to be for more than a decade that Montgomery left behind his spiritual heritage, the personal faith of his missionary parents and the nurture of the Fulneck Moravians. Although he gradually turned his back on the faith of his youth, the reconciling face of Jesus Christ would one day shine upon him again.

Joseph Gales was a man of strong political views and many talents. He combined the vocations of printer, bookseller, auctioneer and newspaper editor. At the time of Montgomery's arrival Gales lived with his family in The Hartshead, a large building then on the edge of the city centre. It served as a shop, the office of *The Register* and the home for the family. It was here that Montgomery took up residence.

The Gales family—Joseph, his wife, and their children, Joseph, Thomas and Sarah (other children were born later)—attended the Unitarian chapel. As there was no Moravian congregation in the city, Montgomery occasionally worshipped with them. Even more occasionally he would visit a Methodist chapel. On the whole, however, James was content to follow the ways of the world, sadly neglecting Christian worship.

Joseph Gales's parents and his three sisters lived in Eckington, then a pleasant village a few miles south of the city. It was Montgomery's delight frequently to walk to Eckington. He was to become closely associated with Gales's sisters, Anne, Elizabeth and Sarah, with whom he worked and later lived for many years.

Montgomery's arrival at the office of *The Register* coincided with the height of the French Revolution (1789–1799). The French government had been an autocratic monarchy. Based on Enlightenment principles, the governmental system underwent a radical change which was accompanied by upheaval and violence. The French king was executed and the

The Hartshead, office and residence of Montgomery until 1836 (from Holland and Everett, *Memoirs of James Montgomery,* vol. 3, 1855, frontispiece)

Napoleonic wars eventually resulted. Opinions and loyalties in England were divided, and many were not averse to referring to the tragic events in France as an argument for change in England. Montgomery refers to the period, writing,

The whole nation at that time was disturbed from its propriety by the example of the revolution in France, nor was there a district in the kingdom more agitated by the passions and prejudges [prejudices] of the day than this. The people of Sheffield, in whatever contempt they may have been led by supercilious censors ignorant of their character, were then as they are now … a reading and thinking people … It was at the height of this great argument that I was led into the thickest of the conflict, though happily for myself under no obligation to take an active part in it.

It was not to be so for the editor of a weekly newspaper. *The Register,* under the leadership of Joseph Gales, advocated radical parliamentary reform. The position of the editor was expressed in plain and fearless terms. Some articles which appeared in 1792–1793 were written by Mrs Gales, described as 'a lady of some taste and talent who rendered her husband efficient assistance in the conduct of the paper'.

The conflict between the Loyalist and the Democratic factions intensified during 1794 and Gales, never a man to sit on the fence, was passionate for reform. He wrote in *The Register* of its aims: 'To rescue my countrymen from the darkness of ignorance and to waken [them] to a just sense of their privilege as human beings'. Joseph Gales became a marked man to those who did not share his views.

By royal decree, 28 February 1794 was declared a 'general fast day'. Reformers in Sheffield chose to honour the day by holding a large public meeting at which there was a prayer, a lecture, and a hymn composed for the occasion by Montgomery. The hymn opens with the following verse; clearly Montgomery was not altogether 'lost in the world'!

O God of Hosts, Thine ear incline,
Regard our prayers, our cause be Thine;
When orphans cry, when babes complain,
When widows weep, canst Thou refrain?

The hymn ends with this plaintive petition to the God whom Montgomery has addressed as 'the King of kings':

Burst every dungeon, every chain,
Give injured slaves their rights again;
Let truth prevail, let discord cease,
The world shall smile in peace.

On 7 April another large public meeting was held on Castle Hill, as a result of which Joseph Gales took his leave of *The Register* and the city. He had written articles for which he was charged with 'seditious libel', and his position and that of his family became too dangerous for him to remain as editor and spokesman for radical political change. However, he wrote stridently in his defence,

To be accused is now to be guilty; and however conscious I may be of having neither done, said nor written anything that militates against peace, order or good government, yet when I am told that witnesses are 'suborned' to swear me guilty of treasonable and seditious practices, it is prudent to avoid such dark assassins and to leave the 'informers' and their employers, the mortification of knowing however deep their villainy was planned, it has been unsuccessful.

With that stirring defence, Gales left the newspaper and the city, both of which he had served with integrity if not with popularity. In 1794, at the age of thirty-three and accompanied by his family, Joseph Gales took refuge in America, where he died in old age in the town of Raleigh, North Carolina. (For a more detailed account of the political scene at the end of the 18th century, see the article by Sarah Groves in Appendix 3.)

The Iris newspaper

What to Joseph Gales was a misfortune was, providentially, an open door for James Montgomery. On 4 July 1794 the first edition of *The Iris* appeared, edited by James Montgomery. The old radical newspaper *The Register* had been purchased by Montgomery for £1,600 and renamed *The Iris*. To find the wherewithal to purchase the presses, types and other working equipment created a considerable difficulty. Benjamin Naylor, a wealthy businessman as well as a Unitarian preacher, came to the rescue. He offered to make available the whole sum required for the purchase of *The Register*.

Chapter 3

The new owners, James Montgomery and Company, announced in the last issue of the old paper the intention of publishing on the following Friday a new Sheffield newspaper, *The Iris*. Thus James Montgomery had, in a few months, been transported from humble assistant to editor and co-owner of a new and less radical weekly newspaper. The published motto of the new paper was: 'Ours are the plans of a fair, delightful Peace, unwarped by party rage, to live as brothers.'

There has been some uncertainty and speculation as to the significance of the name of the new Montgomery paper. Why *The Iris*? Were the beauty and the hue of the iris flower to reflect the strategy of the paper? Or was it because of the new vision and clear-sightedness of the paper that James chose to refer to a part of the human eye? In fact, it was a reference to 'Iris', the goddess who acted as the messenger of the gods whose symbol was the rainbow. The paper's name reflected Montgomery's love of the muse. A poem, 'The Iris', had been received in the editorial office; it began,

O say, art thou the bright-eyed maid,
Saturnia's messenger confest?
Does sacred truth thy mind pervade,
And love celestial warm thy breast?

Although Montgomery did not print this poetic tribute, he did, in the first issue of his paper, set out some principles which were to characterize *The Iris*:

The Editor assures the public that every endeavour will be used to render it worthy of their patronage ... They profess themselves serious to avoid ... the influence of party spirit like others ... they have their own political opinions ... but they have no scruples to declare themselves friends to the cause of peace and reform. It is their wish ... to cherish, as far as they are able, a good opinion of those who differ from them.

So, declared Montgomery, he would edit a newspaper based on fairness and integrity, and with less acrimony and controversy than had characterized *The Register*.

How was he to manage the diverse affairs of the business he had acquired? The sisters of Joseph Gales moved from their village home in Eckington and came to reside at The Hartshead in order to support, advise and assist the young editor-in-chief. Their presence and help was cordially welcomed. Anne and Elizabeth Gales took responsibility for the stationery and bookshop aspects of the enterprise. They were later to be joined by the youngest sister, Sarah. The four, now united in a common purpose, were to remain in mutual friendship for nearly sixty years.

In spite of Montgomery's intention to edit a more moderate and balanced paper, it was not long before he found himself caught up in political controversy. He himself took no active part in public meetings or demonstrations, but some of those who worked for him had no such scruples. Only a month or so after his elevation to the editorial chair of *The Iris* he was persuaded by a visitor to The Hartshead to print some pieces for which he was subsequently to be charged with 'seditious libel' in respect of the war now raging between the England and the French Republic. Although the details of this episode are surrounded by some mystery, Montgomery certainly felt aggrieved.

The title of the offending piece was 'A Patriotic Song, by a Clergyman of Belfast'. The verse which caused the main offence and upon which the case against Montgomery was brought reads,

Europe's fate on the contest's decision depends;
Most important its issue will be,
For should France be subdued, Europe's liberty ends,
If she triumphs the World will be free.

According to the testimony of Montgomery, the song had been published some time before the hostilities began.

As the Sheffield Sessions were imminent, Montgomery was brought before the courts and pleaded 'not guilty'. Nevertheless, the court did find him guilty, but he was allowed bail for the sum of £200. He was brought before the Doncaster Sessions on 22 January 1795. The Doncaster court found Montgomery guilty and pronounced so in the following lurid terms: 'James Montgomery, printer, being a wicked malicious, seditious and evil disposed person ... intending to stir up and excite discontent and sedition among his Majesty's subjects ... and unlawfully to seduce and encourage his said Majesty's subjects to resist and oppose his said Majesty's government and the said war ...'

It is difficult for 21st-century minds to understand such grossly overstated verbiage from 'twelve honest Englishmen' but it was sufficient to commit Montgomery to incarceration in the castle prison in York. He was twenty-three years of age and was to remain in custody for three months, being ordered to pay a fine of £20.

The trial and imprisonment were, of course, a setback and a hardship for Montgomery, but in one sense they worked to his advantage, for many who were politically neutral now regarded him as a Sheffield hero.

As an interesting aside, it is recorded that on the evening before the Doncaster trial, Montgomery had a visitor. It was none other than Joseph Hunt, his employer in Wath-on-Dearne. The visit was a great encouragement to James and he writes, '[the visit] will ever live in the remembrance of him who can forget an injury but not a kindness, no father could have evinced a greater affection ...' James Montgomery was released from York Castle in the middle of April 1795.

Less than one year later, in January 1796, James Montgomery found himself at the centre of a new storm. He was again brought before the Doncaster Sessions, this time on a charge of libel brought by Colonel R. A. Athorpe. A volunteer police force had been formed in the city to deal with rioting and public disturbances. On one notable occasion two citizens had been unlawfully killed by volunteer police under the command of Colonel Athorpe. Naturally, as editor of a local newspaper, Montgomery considered it his duty to comment on this serious disturbance of the peace. The article which he wrote is reproduced in his *Memoirs*. It charged Colonel Athorpe with at least making matters worse by the way in which the volunteers were commanded. The offending part of the article reads,

R A Athorpe, Esq., Colonel of the Volunteers, who had been ... ordered to hold themselves in readiness, now appeared at the head and in a peremptory tone, commanded the people instantly to disperse, which not being immediately complied with, a person ... plunged with his horse among the unarmed, defenceless people, and wounded with his sword men, women and children promiscuously.

York Castle prison

Montgomery was brought before the Barnsley Sessions and was accused of 'false, slanderous and malicious libel on the character of R A Athorpe Esq. a military magistrate'. The charge was eventually referred to the Doncaster Sessions on 21 January 1796. Here Montgomery was sentenced to six months' imprisonment and fined £30, to be paid to the King. Reflecting on this episode later, Montgomery writes,

I was looking over the paper the other day in which the controversy respecting Mr Athorpe is found. There are many terms employed of which I am now ashamed, I [had] resolved when I became an editor, never to commence a personal attack, but should I be attacked, I would repel it with all my might; and this I did in that case.

It would be no exaggeration to say that Montgomery did not take too kindly to his second and longer term of imprisonment in the castle prison in York; it resulted in his suffering intermittent periods of depression. He occupied his long days with writing letters to his friends and concerning himself with the well-being of his newspaper, giving detailed instructions about printing, delivering, and especially about the collection of debts!

Thirty of the letters Montgomery wrote from York are preserved in the Montgomery archives held by Sheffield City Council. We are greatly indebted to Tanya Schmoller, who has been able to reproduce extracts of the Montgomery prison correspondence in her book *Letters from a Newspaperman in Prison*. These letters were written by Montgomery to a friend, J. Pye Smith, who had taken responsibility for the running of *The Iris* for the duration of Montgomery's imprisonment.

J. Pye Smith was the twenty-two-year-old son of a bookseller. He was considered to be one of the most able scholars in Sheffield; later, at the age of twenty-six, he became a lecturer at the prestigious Homerton College. Montgomery, referring to Pye Smith, said, 'This kind friend, when on a certain occasion I had to leave Sheffield for six months, stepped into my place and looked after my affairs.'

The letters which have been preserved are dated January to July 1796 and so cover the whole period of Montgomery's second term of imprisonment. They are all addressed to 'my dear friend'. Three features of this prison correspondence are worthy of comment. The first is the constant anxiety expressed by the writer that The Iris should continue to prosper during his enforced absence. The letters are full of detailed instructions. He writes on 26 January, 'Mr Bradley, bookseller, Chesterfield £3.12.3—write a pressing letter to him and request him not to fail to send the amount by Derby Post.' Three days later he is instructing the staff, 'Don't insert Robbeds' Cough Drops any more at present.' On a personal note he writes in April, 'Give my best respects to Miss G's [sic] who I hope are happy and well ... have you paid the rent? Forgive the inconsistency of these broken sentences; three poor wretches have been hanged today and I am very low spirited.' Secondly, his letters catch the mood of the writer. He writes, 'For my own part, I look back upon the cause of my present misfortune with a kind of gloomy complacency ... As for my future prospects here I feel far less concern than for my affairs at home.' Thirdly, the correspondence from York to Pye Smith shows no concern for his spiritual life and well-being. He seems to have been almost entirely taken up with his predicament and the prosperity of The Iris.

Montgomery was released from York Castle on 5 July 1796. Feeling the need of some recuperation he travelled to Scarborough. He was immediately impressed by the Yorkshire seaside town. He wrote to Joseph Aston in Manchester, a long-standing friend,

On Tuesday last I was liberated from my long and cruel captivity. The same day I arrived at this delightful place. A greater contrast can scarcely be imagined … To me the magnificence of the ocean and the awful grandeur of these winding and mountainous shores are almost entirely new spectacles; for, though I was born in a sea-port, I have never had the opportunity of contemplating such sublime objects since first I came to England at the age of five.

Here in Scarborough, Montgomery was to rest and recover from his ordeal until he could return to his editorial duties in Sheffield in August 1796. There was to be a happy ending to this episode in Montgomery's life. Colonel Athorpe was the presiding magistrate at the Cutlers' Hall in Sheffield, and seeing the *Iris* editor in the crowded court room as an observer one day, beckoned for him to sit beside him on the bench while he wrote a note to be published in the next issue of the paper. There was some reconciliation between the two adversaries.

For the next ten years or so, Montgomery enthusiastically fulfilled his role as editor and owner of *The Iris*. During his Scarborough retreat he had become less than enthusiastic about the partnership with Benjamin Naylor. Schmoller writes, 'It is said that Naylor's policy of neutrality had lost about half of the readership of *The Register*.' Montgomery therefore took the step of dissolving the partnership. This was formalized by Montgomery paying £1,670 for the Naylor share of the business. There may have been another reason for the break. Naylor had fallen in love with a girl who apparently made it a condition of the friendship that Naylor should discontinue his involvement with *The Iris*. Whatever the real reason for the split, it seemed to suit both parties.

Following his return to normal duties, one of the first articles from his pen was entitled 'Prison Amusements'. It was signed by 'Paul Positive', a title Montgomery used frequently. 'Prison Amusements' contained twenty-four pieces, some of which, Montgomery writes, 'were composed in bitter moments and the horrors of the gaol, under the pressure of sickness'. He took up his pen to write 'amusements' as a relief from his 'horrors' and to 'unlock the treasures of the mind'. The collection of pieces was dedicated to Felix Vaughan, the lawyer who had defended Montgomery at his trials. Here is an example of what Montgomery wrote, trifles, as he called them, to release him from the tensions of confinement:

I'm the Lord of all creation—
I—the water wagtail bold!
All around and all you see,
All the world was made for me.

Unthinking, idle, wild and young,
I laughed, and danced, and talked and sung,
And proud of health, of freedom vain,
Dreamt not of sorrow, care or pain,
Concluding in those hours of glee,
That all the world was made for me.

But when the hour of trial came,
When sickness shook this trembling frame,
When Folly's gay pursuits were o'er,
And I could dance and sing no more,
It then occurred how sad 'twould be
Were this world only made for me.

What he had called 'trifles' dedicated to his friend and lawyer were nonetheless a true expression of his gratitude.

In the years following his return to Sheffield, Montgomery occupied himself with editorial work and composing poetry, including one of his most famous poems, 'The Wanderer of Switzerland'. In between his many commitments he found time occasionally to recharge his mind and body with visits to Scarborough. He took up again his love of music-making and even tried his hand at writing a novel. But despite all the calls upon his time, his heart began to yearn for a more solid foundation for the building of his future life.

Personal faith restored

The year 1806 was to see a vital change in the life of James Montgomery. He began to regret some of the vocabulary and expressions he had used in his writing, particularly in his poetry. He now saw them as 'sacrilegious phrases' and 'taking the word of God in vain'. His contacts with the world of the theatre began to trouble him. He writes, 'the manners, characteristics, conversations and incidents which are exhibited at a playhouse are contrary to that purity of heart which the religion of Christ enjoins and requires.' The Lord of heaven was stirring his memory of former and perhaps happier days with the Moravians at Fulneck. Montgomery writes again, 'Up to the year 1806 I occasionally attended theatre but it was with many misgivings. I felt that stage plays were dangerously fascinating amusements.'

Later he tells about a visit to Norfolk Street Chapel in Sheffield, where he heard the funeral sermon for William Bush. 'William was a humble, good Christian … who meekly followed the lowly Jesus.' The occasion made a lasting impression on Montgomery. He tells that a few years before this, in 1802, he had begun to meet occasionally in the 'class meeting' (a group for fellowship, discipleship and teaching) of Charles Clark held in the home of Benjamin Charlesworth; it was here that he was first convicted of his departure from a personal faith. His contact with the vibrant Methodism of Sheffield was to be an important part of his life in the years to come.

Sarah Groves, writing in the *Moravian History Magazine* in 1994, relates that Montgomery had started to read the sermons of John Cennick, the Moravian evangelist whose preaching in the north of Ireland had been the chief means of Montgomery's father coming to his experience of saving faith in the Lord Jesus Christ. From his *Memoirs* it becomes clear that Montgomery had entertained doubts about the reality of a personal faith in Christ. The clouds of these long-held reservations were beginning to clear for the sun of truth to shine.

A further influence at about this time was the outstanding ministry of several well-known preachers who visited Sheffield. The most successful, and perhaps the best known, was William Bramwell, a Wesleyan preacher and revivalist. Bramwell was a Lancastrian with an Anglican background and was the tenth of eleven children. Lacking satisfying fellowship in his Anglican church, he joined the Wesleyan Methodists. After entering the ministry, he travelled the country, preaching powerfully and being the instrument to bring many hundreds to salvation in Christ. Bramwell was a resident minister in Sheffield after 1795 and visited the city regularly in his later itinerant ministry. Montgomery was fortunate to be in Sheffield when Bramwell and others were so influential in the preaching of the gospel. They were spiritual giants of their time.

Faith Cook, in her valuable book *Our Hymn-Writers and their Hymns*, graphically describes Montgomery's return to personal faith. She writes, 'Slowly he was brought sin-burdened and miserable to the Saviour he had long rejected.'

It was not too long before Montgomery turned again towards the place of his boyhood and remembered the days of his youth in the fervent spirituality of his Moravian home. In 1814, now aged forty-three, and with his trust in Christ re-established on the bedrocks of grace and faith, Montgomery applied for membership of the Moravian church at Fulneck. He was readmitted with gladness and joy. The wandering prodigal had returned home, a cause for public celebration in Yorkshire and wherever he was admired. Montgomery wrote his own account of this memorable event in a letter to his brother Ignatius dated 21 December 1814. Extracts from the letter read,

On my birthday (Nov.4.), after many delays and misgivings, and repentings, I wrote to Fulneck for readmission into the Brethren congregation, and on Tuesday, Dec. 6., the lot fell to me in that pleasant place and on Sunday last I was publicly invested with my title to that goodly heritage ... Rejoice with me ... for this unspeakable privilege bestowed on so unworthy and ungrateful a prodigal as I have been ... Particularly remember me ... Tell sister Parminter that I hope to hear her call me brother, and not make an apology.

The words of Scripture with which this chapter begins should have been a salutary warning for Montgomery. If only he had heeded them! They are no less relevant as a warning to all who seek to live a dedicated Christian life in a hostile world.

Wide horizons

LOVE is that name,—for GOD is LOVE!
Here, where, unbuilt by mortal hands,
Mountains below and heaven above,
His awful Temple stands,
I worship:—'LORD! though I am dust and ashes in thy sight,
Be thou my strength; in thee I trust: Be thou my light.'   ('The Peak Mountains', 1812)

I n this chapter we trace some of the people Montgomery knew and the places with which he was associated during the years of his eventful life.

Christian affiliations

After the renewal of his personal faith, the love of God shown to him in Jesus Christ was Montgomery's chief delight and the cornerstone of his work. In the Preface to his *Poetical Works*, written from The Mount, Sheffield, in October 1840, he writes,

I sang of love, the love of my country … I sang likewise of the love of home … I sang of love which man ought to bear to his brother, of every kindred, and every country on the earth … I sang of the love of virtue which elevates man to his true standard under heaven … I sang, too, of the love of God who *is* love … I did not sing in vain.

For the maturing Montgomery, the cross of Christ became the focus of his life as well as the motive for his Christian service. He writes,

1 When to the cross I turn my eyes
And rest on Calvary,
O Lamb of God, my sacrifice,
I must remember Thee.

2 Remember Thee, and all Thy pains,
And all Thy love to me!
Yes, while a breath, a pulse remains,
Will I remember Thee.
('I Will Remember Thee', pub. 1867)

As we have seen, one of Montgomery's earliest contacts in Sheffield was

Joseph Gales, editor of *The Register*. The Gales family worshipped on Sundays at the Unitarian chapel in the centre of the city. As there was no congregation of the Moravian Brethren in Sheffield at that time, Montgomery occasionally worshipped with the Gales family. It may be assumed that, because of his inherited Moravian and Trinitarian background, Montgomery would not have been entirely comfortable in a Unitarian setting. Nevertheless, the relationship between the Gales family and Montgomery was always warm and cordial. Joseph Gales's three sisters became an almost indispensable source of support and stability in the years after Joseph left for America. Until his death in 1854 Montgomery relied heavily on their hospitality and companionship.

Montgomery's Christian sympathies were broad. Even after he was restored to membership of the Moravian congregation at Fulneck, he worshipped regularly with a local Wesleyan church and taught for many years in the large and vibrant Sunday school at Red Hill. The following story was recorded by Dr George Tolley in his 1999 lecture and found in Montgomery's *Memoirs*. Participating in the Red Hill Sunday school was a woman who was over sixty years old but whose education had commenced when she learned the alphabet in the school. She was now able to read, albeit with some hesitation, a chapter from the New Testament. Standing close to the lady, Montgomery took a candle and held it nearby so that she could see more clearly. As Montgomery said afterwards, he was moved and humbled by her achievements.

Montgomery was clear about his own doctrinal position, embracing all the essential aspects of the gospel and adhering closely to the evangelical Moravian teaching. He was, however, generous in his embrace of those who differed from him on issues which he regarded as non-essential. As Dr Tolley says, Montgomery was well received and respected at Methodist, Congregational and Anglican churches. The Calver Street Methodist church and St George's Anglican church, which is now part of the University of Sheffield, saw much of him, especially during special seasons in the Christian calendar. The periods of Lent, Easter and Advent would see Montgomery in attendance at the parish church; at other times he favoured Nonconformity, attending informal Bible study meetings at Methodist churches. He owed much of his spiritual restoration and later development to Anglican and Methodist friends, constantly referring with gratitude to their help and encouragement.

To paraphrase comments by Holland and Everett, they never knew a man of equal Christian spirituality and intelligence whose conduct was so clearly evangelical yet non-sectarian. He joined freely and frequently in public worship with Independents and Baptists.

Theologically, he was unimpressed with high Calvinism. Politically, he was inclined towards the Liberal Party, as opposed to the Tories. Socially, he was a man who could profitably associate with most of his contemporaries. A man for all people, yet a man with discerning judgement.

The end of an era

James Montgomery continued to own and edit *The Iris* until 1825. Matthew Smith had been Montgomery's apprentice for several years and had shown both the ability and loyalty to impress his chief. In 1816, Montgomery announced that he had taken his apprentice into partnership but that the editorship would remain in his hands. The partnership was not to last long. For no known reason, Matthew Smith separated from his former friends and left the city, leaving Montgomery no alternative but to dissolve the partnership.

The Iris continued to be the vehicle to express the editor's views on the issues of the day and the affairs of the city, and to espouse those causes dear to Montgomery. Often he published his thoughts and ideas in the form of poetry. Many poems have been preserved, and some of the longer works appear in Appendix 1.

In 1822, John Blackwell, who had been an accredited Methodist preacher, came to live in Sheffield. Due to ill-health he had resigned as a 'registered minister'. Some years earlier he had been a printer and bookseller in Sheffield. So in 1823 he approached Montgomery with a view to forming a partnership or purchasing *The Iris*. Montgomery replied to the effect that he had no wish to enter into another partnership but, should he decide to retire, he would give John Blackwell first refusal to purchase the paper and the associated business interests.

In June 1825, Montgomery wrote to Blackwell and set out the terms on which he would dispose of the business. These terms were immediately accepted. Tuesday, 27 September 1825 was the last issue of *The Iris* edited by James Montgomery and it contained his address to the readers. Montgomery left his newspaper work to further his widening interests in the affairs of his city and country. It was the end of an era, and of an association which had lasted thirty years. By this time he had stamped his mark not only on the weekly newspaper, but also on his adopted city.

One part of Montgomery's life which did not change then was his domestic situation. He continued to live at the business premises in The Hartshead as he had done for many years. The three Gales sisters also continued to occupy The Hartshead and so were able to supply Montgomery with much-needed home life. This mutually convenient arrangement continued until 1836, by which time Montgomery had occupied the famous building which had been his home and place of business for almost forty years.

'Constantly on the move' (2 Cor. 11:26, NIV)

James Montgomery began his work as a public speaker in 1813. It is perhaps a little surprising that a man so gifted in the written word was apparently so reluctant to appear on a public platform. The occasion was the first anniversary of the formation of the Sunday School Union in Sheffield. He began his address with the words 'My Christian brethren and friends, as we are accustomed to say at Fulneck', which was to become his normal manner of greeting an audience or congregation. He acknowledged the 'great company' gathered and said that the purpose of his talk was to express 'a few sentiments that have deeply impressed my own mind. Christians of sundry denominations are come … in the spirit of peace and good-will … Thus indeed you are proving the sincerity of your professions by the evidence which Christ has himself required, "By this shall all men know that you are my disciples, if ye love one another."' The address was 'long, passionate, eloquent and distinctly Christian'.

Two years later, Montgomery was in Cheshire and was persuaded to preach on the Sunday afternoon. He says he was startled by the idea, replying that he had never before in his life occupied a pulpit in order to preach. In the event, he chose to spend a few minutes alone and then read

Psalm 116, making a few remarks from the notes he had prepared. We are told that the congregation was impressed and Montgomery was persuaded to preach again at the evening service. On this occasion he expounded the Beatitudes (Matt. 5:1–12). According to the writers of the *Memoirs* these were the first and the last times James Montgomery was to be engaged in the ministry of pulpit preaching.

If formal pulpit preaching was not the calling of Montgomery, travelling throughout the country was to become a large part of his life. His journeys were undertaken in order to lecture on a variety of scholarly subjects to learned societies. Other travelling was necessary to engage in missionary or Bible tours in order to educate and encourage fellow-Christians. His commitment to this widening sphere of work began in about 1815 and continued largely unabated until his death in 1854. These itinerant ministries took him to many towns and cities in England, Scotland, Wales and Ireland. A few of these journeys are of particular interest.

One of his early journeys to London was to visit his brother Ignatius in around March or April 1812. He was able to attend the 'May Meetings' of the Moravian Brethren. Ignatius Montgomery was at this time the minister of the Moravian congregation meeting in Fetter Lane. During this visit, James Montgomery was able to attend the anniversary of the Bible Society for the first time. This left an indelible impression on him, and he was to refer to the occasion at several subsequent public meetings. The Bible Society had its origins in Germany, but the British and Foreign Bible Society was established in London in 1804. It was largely supported by Anglicans, its main purpose being to encourage the reading of the Bible. Montgomery became an enthusiastic supporter. Better known, perhaps, is the work of a Welsh Methodist, Thomas Charles of Bala (1755–1814), who was influential in the establishment of the British and Foreign Bible Society.

London had always held a fascination for Montgomery. His visits had not always been entirely happy occasions but he travelled to the capital at least seven times. He gave his opinion: 'London may indeed be the Metropolis of vice but it is the Metropolis of true virtues. If sin abounds there more than elsewhere, grace likewise abounds … and from there is universally diffused through the nation.'

Montgomery was drawn more to the country than to the metropolis, and was more attracted to the rural than to the urban. He writes again, 'Every lover of nature and of the God of nature … prefers the country to the town.'

On 22 May 1830 Montgomery paid another visit to London, this time to deliver a series of popular lectures to the Royal Institution of Great Britain on 'The History of English Literature'. The Royal Institution, founded in 1799, was granted its Charter in 1800 and enlarged by Act of Parliament in 1810. Its objectives, as set out in the Charter, are 'To prosecute scientific and literary research'. Although today we associate the word 'science' with scientists and laboratory work, in the 18th century it was used to refer to knowledge of all kinds.

The subject of these London lectures was, more precisely, 'The Principal British Poets'. To give some idea of the wealth of knowledge which Montgomery had acquired, his lectures were (1) a view of the present state of British poets, (2) general strictures on the earliest British poets from Edward III, (3) poets of the 15–17th centuries, including Donne and Shakespeare, (4) 17th- and 18th-century poets, including Dryden and Milton, (5) the 18th-century poets, including Pope, and (6) an appraisal and appreciation of the well-known works of 18–19th-century poets, including Burns, Cowper, Byron, Coleridge, Wordsworth and Scott.

During this particular visit to London, Montgomery was invited to take part in the Annual Meeting of the London Missionary Society. This was not unusual, for Montgomery had by this time developed a keen interest in the work of foreign missionary societies and he would occasionally travel to attend special events. In 1836 he was present in both Bristol and Exeter for the anniversary services of the Wesleyan Missionary Society, in which he took an active part. His visits to Bristol also enabled him to keep in touch with his brother Ignatius, who was by then a minister in the city. In 1838 Montgomery visited Bristol again, this time to deliver a series of lectures on British poetry similar to those given in London. These lectures were delivered to the Philosophical Society. The welcome and appreciation of Bristolians was no less warm than that of those who heard his London lectures. Their views were printed in a local journal—in popular rhyme, of course!

Thrice welcome to our city, bard beloved!
Patriot and Christian, honoured and approved!
Thou know'st her worth,—hast sung her Reynolds' praise,
In warm and generous, unforgotten lays …
No stranger now, but ever dear— a friend!

It seems that Montgomery had a liking for the work of the artist Sir Joshua Reynolds (1723–1792), who was born in Devon and whose work had won the accolades of the artistic worlds in London and abroad.

Following in the footsteps of the Wesleys in the previous century, Montgomery travelled not only to London and Bristol but also to Newcastle, 'the capital of the north'. On what was, perhaps, his first journey to that city he was persuaded to act as Chairman on the occasion of the anniversary of the Wesleyan Missionary Society. Montgomery began this journey on 30 March 1835 and took in another visit to Fulneck, spending several days there with his Moravian friends.

In conversation Montgomery expressed his views on the great literary scholar Dr Samuel Johnson (1709–1784), a man not always friendly to Nonconformity. He said, 'He … rested his soul at last on the "sure foundation", that is [he] came to Christ as a humble and sincere penitent and obtained mercy through the atonement.' If that was true of Johnson, it was equally true of Montgomery. So it was not only an endorsement of Dr Johnson's Christian faith, but also a testimony to his own.

Montgomery visited Newcastle again in March 1836 to deliver the six now famous lectures on British poets. (They were to be given again in Manchester in the same year.) James Everett tells of a piece of typical Montgomery wit. As he and Montgomery passed through Newcastle's meat market, Everett pointed to the fine specimens of beef on display. Montgomery said, 'I dare say they are excellent but I am no judge of meat … never having purchased six penny-worth in all my life—no, not even when I kept house in York Castle.'

The now famed lecture series was published under the lengthy title of *Lectures on General Literature, Poetry etc. Delivered to the Royal Institution in 1830 and 1831 in One Volume and Published in New York (1840)*. Apparently, even in six lectures there were more things

Montgomery would have liked to say but time was against him. So in the Preface to the published version he writes, 'The lectures have been anxiously revised, especially those parts which the limited time allowed for delivery required to be omitted on the spot, but which appeared to be more necessary for their intelligence when submitted to cool perusal, than when uttered before indulgent hearers with the living voice.' That piece of typical Montgomery prose illustrates the rather verbose style of even gifted writers and speakers in the 19th century!

Montgomery's travels were not always working journeys; there were also some periods for leisure. He occasionally found time to relax in England's famous spa towns. His *Memoirs* mention times free from work when he visited Bath, Buxton, Harrogate and Matlock, usually for relaxation and often accompanied by one or more of his many friends. On one early visit to Buxton in 1812 he was fortunate enough to be present in the town at the consecration of the new parish church by the Lord Bishop of Lichfield and Coventry. He described the church as 'a very elegant and very commodious edifice founded by the late Duke of Devonshire and capable of seating nearly a thousand people'. He concluded a letter written on the day of the ceremony, 'I am better in health and more cheerful than when I came hither, thank God'. The bracing Buxton air had lightened his spirits.

The Montgomery *Memoirs* refer to journeys undertaken by him and described as missionary tours. These were for the purpose of speaking at missionary society meetings, or simply to encourage missionary work in which he now had an increasing interest. He visited Derbyshire in 1822, Halifax in 1825, York and Stockport in 1828, Manchester in 1831 and Newcastle in 1835. He was in Bristol and Exeter again for missionary gatherings in 1831, and as part of a Moravian missionary celebration he joined his brethren in Birmingham in the same year.

An extensive missionary tour of Scotland was arranged for him in 1841. This took him to Glasgow, Irvine, his home town, Kilmarnock, Stirling, Perth, Dundee and Edinburgh. The tour of Scotland was particularly poignant for Montgomery, as he writes to his friend, George Bennett, 'In the beginning of June I am engaged to accompany our friend Peter La Trobe on a missionary visit to Scotland, my native country, on which I have not set foot since the year 1776, when as a child I was transported to Ireland.' In fact, the tour of Scotland had to be curtailed by a few weeks due to the illness of his companion. A similar tour was undertaken in the following year, this time to Ireland, firstly to Dublin and then to Belfast. Unfortunately, the references to missionary tours in the *Memoirs* are more concerned with dates and places visited than with the content of Montgomery's many addresses. It would be enlightening, to say the least, to know what contributions he made to the meetings he attended. It is remarkable that there is no mention of any visit to the Moravian settlement at Gracehill, where Montgomery spent the earliest years of his life. Maybe there were by now no familiar brethren with whom he could renew acquaintance.

Other Montgomery journeys are described as Bible tours. He visited Stratford-upon-Avon in 1819 for special meetings of the Bible Society, and toured much of the north of England in 1827 on what was described as 'a Bible Tour to encourage the understanding of the Bible'. This was followed two years later by similar visits to the Lake District and Yorkshire. Yet again the *Memoirs* are frustratingly brief about what took place on what were for Montgomery important events. His visit to Stratford-upon-Avon in 1819 was for the purpose of forming a branch of the Bible Society in Shakespeare's town. He tells us that he was deeply affected by the occasion, there being, as he spoke, a picture of the actor and playwright David Garrick before him and one of William Shakespeare behind him, both painted by Joshua Reynolds. Unfortunately, we are not told what Montgomery spoke about, but it would be difficult to believe that no mention was made of the two worthy gentlemen. He tells us that the collection at the meeting amounted to £50, a significant sum of money in those days!

Montgomery's visit to York in 1828 was for the purpose of presiding at the Wesleyan Missionary Society anniversary service. On this occasion he was unwell and unable to finish his talk. He remarked that he was unlike Bunyan's Pilgrim, who was at least able to finish his journey!

Of all the places which Montgomery frequently visited, Ockbrook near Derby was one of his favourites. Ockbrook, like Gracehill in Ireland and Fulneck in Yorkshire, was a Moravian settlement built on a similar plan to that of Herrnhut, Zinzendorf's Moravian establishment in Saxony. It too was set on high land, also as a 'city on a hill'. Ockbrook consisted of a chapel, schools, cottages, a shop, lecture hall, manse and burial ground. The impressive group of buildings was clustered round the chapel and built in 1751–1752. There are five recorded occasions when Montgomery visited Ockbrook to foster his growing fondness for the Moravians and all they stood for. On May Day 1841, he visited Ockbrook with his brother Robert. Their brother Ignatius had died there just a few days earlier. Montgomery told John Holland, 'I am going to Ockbrook … my poor brother is in heaven.' Ignatius Montgomery, four years younger than James, had been a Moravian minister from 1808, when he was thirty-two years old. He had served the Moravian cause as a 'labourer' and minister at Gracehill, Ockbrook, London and Bristol. He retired because of ill-health in 1818 and returned to Ockbrook three years later. He spent the last years of his life as an invalid and was cared for by Mary Agnes, his devoted wife. The death of Ignatius Montgomery in 1841 was announced as follows: 'At Ockbrook, near Derby on 29th ultimo, Rev Ignatius Montgomery, formally a minister of various congregations of the United Brethren in Ireland and England, having found grace to prove himself a good and faithful servant through long labours and longer suffering entered into the joy of the Lord at the age of 65 years.'

As was to be expected, perhaps, Ignatius's widow requested James to prepare a description of his brother's character which was to be read by the Ockbrook minister at the 'love feast' held the day after the funeral. A few days later, James and Robert visited Fulneck in preparation for an extended tour of Scotland with Peter La Trobe.

Montgomery returned to Wath-on-Dearne for sentimental visits in 1820 and 1847. In 1835 and 1839, he visited Wentworth House at the invitation of Earl Fitzwilliam. On the latter occasion, the Earl apparently wished to discus with Montgomery the possibility of relocating the Sheffield Infirmary to another, more favourable site. Montgomery strenuously opposed the idea, although we are unfortunately not told on what grounds.

Given the zeal of the Moravians for evangelism, it is unfortunate that Montgomery's *Memoirs* are silent on the influence he had on the lives of individuals apart from those who were his close friends. It would have added a valuable dimension to the Montgomery story if something was known about those who were converted to Christ as a result of his ministry. It may be that modesty restrained him from writing or even speaking of such matters. The benefit of the doubt must be given to him, especially to one who could use his pen to show his heart:

When bound with sins and trespasses,
From wrath we fain would flee,
Lord, cancel our unrighteousness,
And set the captives free.   ('The Soul's Aspiration', pub. 1867)

Friendships

THE GALES SISTERS

During his long and active life in Sheffield, Montgomery forged a large number of friendships. There can be no doubt that his life was enriched by the sisters of Joseph Gales. They have been mentioned previously because hardly any aspect of Montgomery's life was not touched by these gifted and honourable women. They had left the comfort of their family home in Eckington to join Montgomery at The Hartshead, not only to support his work with *The Iris*, but also to provide him with the only home life he was to enjoy.

Their move to The Hartshead occurred in 1794. There they lived and worked in mutual respect and comparative comfort until they moved to The Mount in 1836. Their new home was part of a palatial gentleman's residence in the Broomhill district, a desirable suburb of Sheffield.

In 1821, Elizabeth Gales sadly died; she was described by Montgomery as 'the first loss' in the closely knit 'family'. They had been associated for almost thirty years, and Montgomery felt the loss deeply. Elizabeth was 'a fine looking woman, frank in her manners … engaged with others in some of the benevolent institutions'. She was buried near her parents in the churchyard at Eckington. On leaving the committal service, Montgomery, speaking, as it were, to his departed friend, was heard to say, 'Betsy, when I die, bury *me* here.'

Chapter 4

Anne Gales, the eldest sister, died after the move to The Mount. She had suffered from increasing dementia for several years. Christmas 1837 was a sad and trying time rather than a joyful occasion. Montgomery watched over his friend, wept, prayed and read to her from 'the word God furnishes for such a time'. 'We have lived together,' Montgomery writes, 'for more than forty years and never did I receive from her one unkind word ... we have sometimes differed in opinion but she was oftener [*sic*] right than I was.' His tribute to his lifelong friend was, as would be expected, in the form of verse. The poem was entitled 'In Memory of My Dear Friend Anne Gales' and dated 24 February 1838. The first and the last verses read,

She went as calmly as at eve
A cloud in sunset melts away,
While blending lights and shadows weave
The winding-sheet of dying day ...

'Good night!' once more;—when next we meet,
May this our salutation be,
'Good morrow!' at the judgement seat,
'Good morrow!' to eternity.

Sarah Gales, the youngest of the three sisters, outlived Montgomery and was his companion at The Mount until he died in 1854. The relationship was always one of respect and affection, but nothing more. Twenty years after Joseph Gales and his family left Sheffield for America, Sarah decided to visit her distant family who were now living in Washington. Montgomery accompanied her to Liverpool to see her aboard *The Lancaster*. Asked by a friend how he felt having parted from 'his charge', Montgomery replied in a typically cryptic manner, 'as happy as despair can make me'. Sarah Gales was a literary figure in her own right, being the editor of a small periodical, *The Portfolio*, which circulated among a group of her friends. She fulfilled the role of housekeeper at both The Hartshead and The Mount. Montgomery wrote to her during one of his visits to Buxton in 1822, 'We are doing as well as we can without you and shall

Sarah Gales (from Holland and Everett, *Memoirs of James Montgomery,* vol. 6, 1856, frontispiece)

gladly continue to do so as long as you can enjoy yourself and do without us.' The letter is signed simply, 'Your friend, J Montgomery'.

Montgomery regarded himself as a 'pastor' to the household. On the occasion of a visit by Sarah to Buxton, he wrote, 'I was sorry that I did not give you, as a daily companion, our Text Book. I enclose a copy which will speak comfortably to you in the words of eternal life, whenever you look into it; and as a morning and evening star, the two texts of each day will shine from heaven upon your mind, both when you rise and when you lie down.'

Montgomery and Sarah Gales were in frequent correspondence whenever duty or relaxation caused their separation. The letters show tender concern one for the other, but none of them indicates more than a healthy friendship and a desire for mutual well-being. Sarah was to remain with Montgomery until his death, a faithful companion to the end.

DANIEL PARKEN

Parken was a London-based barrister who corresponded with Montgomery for some years, particularly between 1806 and 1812. The friendship centred around their literary interests, although a Christian faith and doctrinal beliefs underpinned their relationship. Parken was born in Dunstable and educated for the bar. In 1805, he succeeded Revd Samuel Greathead as the editor of the *Eclectic Review*, a periodical later to be edited by the more famous hymn-writer Josiah Conder. The *Eclectic Review* was, as the name implies, a magazine devoted to the expression and critique of philosophical, scientific and literary ideas chosen from broad and non-sectarian sources. As such it appealed to Montgomery and editors like Parken and Conder.

Probably one of the earliest letters from Montgomery to Daniel Parken is dated July 1806 and was written during a period when James Montgomery was re-establishing his personal faith. It begins, 'Dear Sir' and ends, 'I am very truly your obliged friend'. In October of the same year, the address is much more cordial—'Dear Friend'—and the letter is signed, 'I am truly your affectionate Friend'.

The matter which had originally drawn the two friends together was Montgomery's idea to erect a monument to the memory of Lord Nelson in

The Mount, Broomhill, Sheffield; the home of James Montgomery from 1836 until his death (from Holland and Everett, *Memoirs of James Montgomery,* vol. 6, 1856, frontispiece)

Sheffield. The sculptor was to be Sir Francis Chantry, and the eight-foot-high bronze statue was to cost £450. Montgomery wrote an appeal to the people of Sheffield, commending the project for which he had a personal interest. Parken commented that if his appeals for the project had any fault, it was that they were too long; at the same time, however, they were so 'interesting' that he could not 'mutilate them'.

Montgomery's first contribution to the *Eclectic Review* was published in 1807. The subject was 'The Life of Colonel Hutchinson', Hutchinson being the Governor of Nottingham Castle during the Civil War.

Parken lived most of his life in London, working as a barrister in Lincolns Inn. He died in Aylesbury in July 1812 after a brief illness following a road accident. The accident, illness and death of his friend was communicated to Montgomery by a Mr Beddows in a letter dated 24 July 1812. Beddows says of Parken, 'I need not describe him to you, who knew him so well.' In a conversation soon after Parken's death, Montgomery expressed the view that Parken was 'a religious man', presumably meaning that he was a Christian. Montgomery had written a letter to Parken which he never received; in it he alluded to the 'rest and communion of the Saints'. He regarded Parken as a scholar and academic as well as a Christian. Parken's work as a barrister was successful, although Montgomery regarded his court manner as being more solid than eloquent. With Parken's death, Montgomery's career as a contributor to the *Eclectic Review* was over. Referring to his friendship with Parken in a letter to his brother Ignatius, Montgomery wrote that, although he was distressed at Parken's death, he was not in despair. 'God is only humbling me under His mighty hand, O how mysterious are His ways [judgements]. My dear friend Parken *now* knows, though we know not, why he was unexpectedly removed from us.'

GEORGE BENNETT

One of Montgomery's closest friends was George Bennett. He was a man like Montgomery, holding his views thoughtfully but strongly, a man of high moral principles, a Christian by confession, an evangelical by persuasion, and with a zeal for missionary endeavour. There was hardly any Christian or benevolent cause which George Bennettt, who was attached to an Independent Congregational church in Sheffield, did not support with all his considerable influence. He was a Christian gentleman in the Montgomery mould. In Bennett, Montgomery found a stable, wise and faithful counsellor and friend.

An incident involving Bennett in 1814 shows Montgomery in rather a strange light. It will be remembered that Montgomery had returned to the assurance of faith in Christ in about 1805–1806. Yet eight years or so later he was somewhat reticent about approaching the Lord's Table. The occasion in question was the first anniversary of the West Riding branch of the London Missionary Society (LMS), in which both Bennett and Montgomery were actively engaged. Montgomery spoke enthusiastically at this meeting, showing the kind of zeal that his parents had for the work of evangelism abroad. At one of these LMS meetings, it was arranged for the ministers and speakers to gather at the communion table for the sacrament as it was observed among the Independents. Montgomery, invited by George Bennett to attend, expressed his reluctance: 'I am afraid I am not a Christian'; to which his friend replied, 'let your Christian friends be the judges as they may be better able to decide dispassionately, than yourself'. Eventually Bennett persuaded Montgomery to take part, which he did 'with fear and trembling'. This reticence is curious for a man who by now was firmly established in his own personal faith in Christ and was regarded so by his friends and fellow-worshippers. We will never know what it was in Montgomery's heart that made him fear as he did. Maybe there is a clue contained in an address he gave only a month earlier to a meeting of the Sheffield Sunday School Union. He concluded, 'We may have a name among Christians; we may be affected by the solemnity of Divine worship, we may delight in the joy and animation of meetings like this and yet be devoid of the spirit of power and Godliness'. Montgomery set a very high standard of Christian piety and behaviour for himself and his fellow-Christians. To feel 'unworthy' to attend at a communion service may have been the passing 'feeling' of a man who longed to be more holy and like his Saviour. It is certainly a strange event, but one which can teach us much about the seriousness of true discipleship.

Both Bennett and Montgomery were committed to the furtherance of education. Through his friendship with Bennett, Montgomery was enlisted to support the Rotherham Independent College (later the Masborough Institute), an academy for learning established in 1795 and located in Masborough. The foundation of the college was funded by Joshua Walker, a wealthy industrialist and foundry owner. The academy was 'for the education of young men who had devoted their lives to the Christian ministry amongst Congregational [Independent] churches'. A report from the Masborough Institute for 1815 and prepared by Montgomery commemorates the death of Joshua Walker. He said,

> We are commanded to love the Lord our God supremely, and to love him only; it follows, that we must serve him in the same manner that we love him, with all our heart and mind and strength; with all the corporeal and intellectual faculties, with all our affections and all our attainments. The Independent churches … for a long period, have proved by experience the benefit of being served by pastors who, while they are led by the Spirit of God into the knowledge of the truths necessary for salvation, have also been instructed [in] those estimable branches of human learning which enlarge, enlighten, ennoble, and enrich the understanding, the imagination, the feelings, and the judgement.

This extract from his address indicates Montgomery's style of oratory, brings out those things which he valued, and is quite a rare example of his recorded public speaking.

The *Memoirs* describe Bennett as one of Montgomery's most intimate friends, yet they were separated for several years by Bennett's call to serve the Lord in the South Sea Islands with the London Missionary Society. He sailed in May 1821 with his colleague, Daniel Tyerman. He returned eight years later, to the intense joy of Montgomery. This temporary parting of the ways was an occasion for Montgomery to write to 'My friend, George Bennett, Esq., of Sheffield',

Go; take the wings of morn,
And fly beyond the utmost sea;
Thou shalt not feel thyself forlorn,
Thy God is still with thee;
And where His Spirit bids thee dwell,
There, and there only, thou art well.

This may not be Montgomery at his best, but it is not entirely untypical.

On his return, Bennett landed at Deal on 5 June 1829. He wrote immediately to Montgomery, 'This is my dear, my native land, bless the Lord oh my soul'. At the time of Bennett's return to Sheffield, Montgomery was in Keswick on one of his missionary tours. He wrote to Bennett, ending his letter in typical fashion: 'God bless you! Yea, and you shall be blessed. I am truly your affectionate friend, changed only as the years have changed me.'

George Bennett died on 19 November 1841 aged sixty-eight. Montgomery was preparing to travel to Birmingham when he learned of the unexpected death of his friend caused by a stroke suffered as he journeyed from Hackney to London.

The following lines were penned by Montgomery to his friend when Bennett prepared to visit Tahiti, where Christianity had recently been established. It shows the deep spiritual bond between the two men.

Thus then in peace depart,
And angels guide thy footsteps:—No!
There is a feeling in the heart,
That will not let thee go:
Yet go,—thy spirit stays with me;
Yet go,—my spirit goes with thee.

JOSEPH ASTON

Montgomery's friendship with Joseph Aston was conducted chiefly by correspondence. In modern jargon, they were pen pals! Joseph Aston was the son of a gun-maker whose business was based in Manchester. Aston followed his father into business until he 'retired' early to follow the pursuits of politics and journalism.

He was described, in later life at least, as 'kindly, amiable ... articulate and popular'. He was also a figure of substance in the field of literature, having established a profitable bookselling business in Manchester.

He was ten years older than his friend Montgomery, having been born in 1761. Their relationship, lasting though it proved to be, was not always cordial. There were occasions when each expressed some disappointment with the other. In 1823, Aston complained that Montgomery had not spent very much time with him on a visit to Manchester. Montgomery replied 'To Aston, Bookseller, Manchester' in a letter dated 10 April 1823, writing, 'Your letter has wounded me very unexpectedly on a matter where I imagined I was perfectly secure from causing you pain.' He goes on to explain that the visit to Manchester which was the cause of Aston's complaint was necessary to fulfil some 'painful duty'. He asserts that he did spend four and a half hours with his Manchester friend. He signs the letter, rather abruptly for Montgomery, 'Your faithful and obliged friend'.

Where the two men joined warmly together was on the subject of poetry. Aston could be an attractive poet. Even so, Montgomery's view of some of Aston's work was that, with his cultured voice, he could read poetry better than he could compose it. In rather more friendly fashion he commented that reading poetry well is a rarer gift than writing. In a conversation with John Holland, Montgomery observed with reference to his friend Aston,

> He was an early friend of mine and many letters passed between us. This was at a time when I was not burdened or fearful of correspondence. I told him all that was on my heart, and a great deal more than I ought to have told any person in the world; these letters may some day rise up in judgement against me.

After the death of Joseph Aston, Montgomery's letters were returned to the writer, and no harm was done. He was tempted, Montgomery says, to destroy them. Instead, no longer fearing the rising judgment, he gave them to the authors of the *Memoirs*, who comment, rightly, that the extensive use made of them in the *Memoirs* justifies the view that they were of great interest and entirely unobjectionable! What concerned Montgomery was that the correspondence should not become a matter of idle speculation by those few people who might misuse them. The letters chosen to be included in the *Memoirs* show little about which Montgomery would be embarrassed. He had a sensitive nature, more ready to build up than to pull down, whether in correspondence or conversation.

What is believed to be the last letter Montgomery wrote to Joseph Aston was addressed to the *Recorder* Office in Rochdale. This letter expresses some regret that Aston had complained about Montgomery's 'long silence'. It is possible, however, that this 'last letter', dated 1827, is not really the last communication between Montgomery and Aston. Joseph Aston died in Chadderton Hall, Manchester, in 1843 at the age of eighty-two. It is hardly likely that he and Montgomery had no correspondence between 1827 and 1843. The 'last letter' referred to ended, 'Give my kindest regards to Mrs Aston, and [I] assure you of my unchanging and unchangeable sentiments of affection.' It was signed simply, 'Your Friend'.

Aston's daughter visited Montgomery the year after her father died. This friendly visit was followed by a letter to her in which Montgomery commented that he was glad to have had the friendship of Joseph Aston during 'the most perilous and painful period of my life'. He continues, 'I was harassed almost to despondency concerning my state before my Creator, Redeemer and Judge for having forsaken that communion of his people amongst whom I was born.' He goes on, 'Now your father for several years of this sore trial, having been the only friend with whom I could freely correspond, my letters to him were so purely personal and confidential, that they were the very last disclosures of my soul ...' This affectionate letter ends, 'For your kindness, and the daughter of my dearest friend, I am glad to subscribe, truly, your much obliged friend.' Whatever occasional disagreements had occurred between the friends, there is no doubt that there was a lasting warmth and admiration between them.

Causes and effects

He comes, with succour speedy,	To give them songs for sighing,
To those who suffer wrong;	Their darkness turn to light;
To help the poor and needy,	Whose souls, in bondage lying,
And bid the weak be strong;	Were precious in His sight.

('Christ's Reign', pub. 1867)

This inspiring verse is often printed in modern hymn-books as part of the familiar hymn 'Hail to the Lord's Anointed', which was inspired by Psalm 72. It is possible also to recognize echoes from the 'Nazareth manifesto' recorded in Luke 4:18–21. In fact, Montgomery's verse comes from another hymn which is not so well known and is entitled 'Christ Reigns'. It expresses quite perfectly Montgomery's loyalty to the gospel as believed by the Moravians and which inextricably links fervent saving faith with an abundance of 'good works'.

Politics

Late in his life, Montgomery attended a rather boisterous meeting in Sheffield Town Hall convened to raise subscriptions for the 'poor and needy' folk in the city. In his address he said, 'for my part, I have long been convinced that, "This is the way God's gifts to use, first enjoy and then diffuse."'

Despite Montgomery's enlightened enthusiasm for alleviating suffering, especially in his later life, he was never committed to party politics. He says, 'I sometimes dipped into political controversy; but politics became more and more disagreeable to me. I enter no further into them than my duty as an editor compels me to do. I wish I had nothing to do with them.' He was, of course, referring to politics and policies, not to the people who happened to be politicians.

In 1837 he paid a visit to John Holland, intimating that he was about to reveal a secret ('No, I am not going to tell you that I am about to be married'). The 'secret' turned out to be a request for him to stand for Parliament. He did not take up the opportunity, although he did, at this time, align himself with the politics generally known as 'conservative'. It was never a binding attraction.

Abolition of slavery

A cause in which Montgomery became deeply involved was the anti-slavery campaign. His name is not as readily associated with the movement as those of William Wilberforce and John Newton, but in his own city he was a powerful advocate of abolition. His influence was applied by means of articles in *The Iris*, speaking at abolitionist meetings and in a wealth of personal correspondence. Reports he received from Moravian sources in the West Indies fuelled his opposition to the slave trade. His own parents, during their missionary work in the West Indies, had devoted much of their time to working among the 'outcasts from hope and humanity'. The anti-slavery poem 'The West Indies' is considered in Appendix 1.

The abolitionist cause had begun long before Montgomery was in a position to bring his influence to bear on the matter. It is remarkable that his birth in 1771 coincided with the infamous case of the ill-treatment of a black man in the west of England which brought the comment that 'slaves could not breathe in England'.

Sympathy for the African slaves transported to the West Indies aroused emotional sympathy, 'fashionable feelings', as they were sometimes described. For Montgomery, the opposition to trading in slaves was a deeply held conviction and principle which would not allow him to remain silent or inactive. He wrote in *The Iris* as early as 1805, 'To what wickedness—to what misery are we akin [associated]? No;—The sufferer is our brother, his worldly oppression denies our consanguinity [blood relationship], yet, the Negro is assuredly related to all the rest of the human race.'

The considerable political and social pressures eventually resulted in the British Act for the Abolition of Slavery which received Royal Assent in August 1833. Slavery as it was then practised was to cease in 1840. Shortly after this memorable victory for freedom, Montgomery presided at a meeting where about 500 Christian friends listened to an address during which the unnamed speaker held before the people a large placard on which he had printed 'Slavery abolished, August 1834—Thank God'. He ended his address, 'To God our thanks are especially due on this occasion, for this glorious event He has wrought; for the abolition of slavery was not attributed to either patriotic politicians or to poets, but to Christians in their character ...' 'Slavery and Christianity could not exist together,' added Montgomery.

The impetus for the abolition of slavery was the earlier bill of 1805 which was passed by the Commons and blocked in the House of Lords. Wilberforce, Charles Fox and others eventually persuaded the Lords to accept the legislation. The bill became law on 25 March 1807 and effectively banned slavery in all British colonies. It was not until 1833, however, that Parliament passed the Slavery Abolition Act. This defining act was designed to ban slavery worldwide and was to be the lasting legacy of William Wilberforce. James Montgomery was one of many earnest evangelical leaders who actively promoted the anti-slavery campaigns. John Wesley had seen the need for reform in his time; his last preserved letter, dated February 1791, is worth quoting for its brevity and intensity on the subject: '... a man who has a black skin, being wronged or outraged by a white man, can have no redress; it being the law, in all our colonies, that the oath of a black against a white goes for nothing. What villany [sic] is this!' To that, Montgomery would say 'Amen'.

Climbing boys

In July 1807, Montgomery wrote a letter to his friend Daniel Parken, editor of the *Eclectic Review*, in which he advised him that he would shortly receive reviews of Robert Southey's *Specimens of British Poets* and William Wordsworth's *Lyrical Ballads*. These were eventually received by Parken, with an added request that he should also include a reference to the story 'The Chimney Sweeper's Boy' by Samuel Roberts. This had made a deep impression on Montgomery and he wrote, 'I assure you it has affected me to tears more than once in reading it—and it was only written to do good and does not pretend to be poetry.' This was the first occasion when Montgomery recorded his sympathy for the boys, some of them as young as four or five, who spent their lives as 'climbing boys' up and down the dark recesses of chimneys.

Holland and Everett write, '… of that degraded and suffering class of children—chimney sweepers—Montgomery was the friend and advocate. For over ten years he championed their cause in *The Iris* and at every opportunity sought to bring their dirty occupation to an end.'

On their behalf Montgomery put his pen to paper and to poetry:

If Chimneys *must* be swept, and if they *can only* be swept by friction of the bones and muscles of infants, are the feelings of an exquisitely sensitive frame necessary to this coarse operation?

Does it require the energies of an intellectual, as an immortal spirit within the living machine, to dislodge a little soot from the hollow of a vile funnel? No, certainly; and the practice would be infinitely improved by employing the bodies of dead children in the process, to be worked up and down the chimney with ropes, like the bundle of straw in the old method, by a man at the top and another at the bottom, like a pair of sawers.

Fortunately, to avoid any possible misunderstanding of the irony, Montgomery explains, 'This idea was suggested with deliberation, because it would fill every mind with unutterable horror.'

Although chimney sweeps were usually boys (hence 'climbing boys'), occasionally it came to light that young girls were also used. Montgomery relates the occasion in about 1824 when, after an Easter climbing boys' dinner (an occasion to raise funds), a girl was introduced to him by her parents; she had come to the dinner with the boys. When the parents were charged with 'barbarous conduct', they replied that they had no boys and, being destitute, they employed their daughter to sweep.

In 1840 the employment of climbing boys to sweep chimneys became illegal. Unfortunately, as Anthony Lacey writes, this legislation was not enforced. In 1864 a further act was passed to tighten the law, but it was not until 1875 that it became illegal to sweep chimneys without police approval and that this was enforced. John Wood has written that 'A good deal of credit for promoting public awareness of the plight of climbing boys must go to Charles Kingsley through his 1863 novel *Water Babies*.'

The General Infirmary

What is now the Sheffield Royal Infirmary was built in the city centre in 1792. It was originally called the Sheffield General Infirmary and was given its new name in 1897. It was closed in 1980. Many of its unusual features contributed to its distinctive appearance. An outpatients department, added in 1884, was designed as an octagonal structure with a crowning cupola on a roof of wrought-iron lattice girders. It was significantly extended in 1900, with a nurses' home built in the grounds on Infirmary Road. Perhaps not surprisingly, part of the site is now occupied by a supermarket.

The first stone of the original building was laid on 4 September 1792. It was designed 'For the sick and lame and poor of all nations'. Dated vocabulary perhaps, but with a 21st-century ring? Montgomery was an observer at the ceremony, part of a large crowd gathered for this auspicious event. Little did he realize that in later years he would occupy the influential position of President of the Board of Managers of the hospital. As editor of a local newspaper, Montgomery followed the progress of the building with pertinent comments designed to interest the public in giving towards the cost of buildings and furnishings.

The theatrical world of Sheffield added its own contribution to the cost of the project by performing a comedy entitled *The Wonder*. Montgomery was present at the performance. His closing oration included the following:

… Thrice happy you! Because the poor are blest
For every smile that cheers this happy place
Shall kindle comfort into a mourner's face!
Some pleasures sting—but this shall leave behind
A sweet memorial, soothing to the mind …

In 1838 Montgomery presided over a special meeting of the General Board of Governors which was convened to consider a proposal to build a 'House for Fever Patients' as an addition to the Infirmary. This project found favour with Montgomery's friend Earl Fitzwilliam, who donated £500 from the family at Wentworth House. The building, which became known as an Isolation Hospital, was completed in 1839. Architects and builders in those days seemed able to design and construct complex and substantial buildings much more quickly than in our own more regulated order today. With less sophisticated equipment than we have today, those 19th-century builders completed their work in an admirably short time-scale.

Montgomery, in his inimitable way, had a poem for the advent of the hospital. It was entitled, 'At a Sermon for an Infirmary'. Here are some of his lines.

Through paths of loving-kindness led,
Where Jesus triumphed, we will tread;
To all, with willing hands dispense
The crumbs of our benevolence:
Hark! The voice of Pity calls
Misfortune to these hallowed walls;
The breaking heart, the wounded breast,
And helpless poverty distressed …
Here the whole family of woe
Shall friends, and home, and comfort know …
This favoured mansion deign to bless:
The cause is *Thine*,—oh, send success.

The Mechanics Library

Sheffield has been world famous for its steel production and mechanical engineering, although these industries have been decimated in recent times. In 1824 a number of the city's influential citizens met with leaders of industry to discus the formation of a library for the use of engineering managers, their workforces and apprentices. Montgomery was quick to see the advantages of such an enterprise and was in the vanguard of the project. With his customary enthusiasm he argued that a little learning could be dangerous, but that it was a privilege, if not a duty, for every individual to get as much learning as he or she could. He did not hesitate to accept the office of president of the newly formed Sheffield Mechanics Library.

In February 1825 he wrote to the committee of the library, showing the extent of his commitment: 'I am very unwell today and yet I am obliged to travel out of town. I have stipulated that I shall return this evening for the meeting.' He goes on to congratulate the members of the committee on their appointment. The lengthy letter ends, 'Accept my assurances of my sincere respect and so far as I can serve the Institution, you may always command the services of your friend, James Montgomery.'

His interest in and support of the library included the giving of several lectures, usually on some appropriate literary theme, as well as acting assiduously as the chairman of the working committee. In 1853 he finally relinquished his involvement and was honoured in the following address by the Secretary:

The members of this library have … felt it to be highly honoured to have the name of James Montgomery as the head of their list of officers and friends. Mr Montgomery took an active part in the affairs of the library in the maturity of his days and intended his presence here this evening to furnish renewed proof of his … interest in this Institution. May the recollection of the past be a source of consolation to him in his retirement and may the anticipation of the future shed … a serenity on his remaining days.

They really knew how to make a man feel appreciated in those days, even if the tributes tended to be somewhat drawn-out!

Missionary evangelism

The departure of Montgomery's parents to the West Indies when he was young and impressionable brought a deep sense of loss. It also later proved to be a source of inspiration. As we have seen, he became missionary-minded, with the heart if not the calling of an evangelist. The history of modern missions does not begin with William Carey in 1791, as is sometimes asserted; John Wesley had encountered a Moravian missionary expedition on his way to Georgia in 1735. The Moravians were a missionary people with an unquenchable zeal for the evangelization of the lost wherever they were to be found.

As a Moravian, James Montgomery had been nurtured in this missionary tradition and it endured throughout his life. His support of foreign missions found him engaged in 'missionary tours' throughout the country, attending meetings of missionary societies and lending his support to many missionary and evangelistic causes. Though he had not been called to this demanding work, he was aware, from his missionary companions, of what it meant to 'forsake all' and for Christ's sake 'go'.

Perhaps Montgomery's missionary zeal and the feeling he had for the cost involved in a missionary call can best be appreciated from the following verses from a poem simply entitled, 'Farewell to a Missionary':

Home, kindred, friends and country, these
Are things with which we never part;
From clime to clime, o'er land and seas,
We bear them with us in our hearts;
And yet 'tis hard to feel resigned,
When they must all be left behind.
But when the pilgrim's staff we take,
And follow Christ from shore to shore,
Gladly for Him we all forsake,
Press on, and only look before;
Though humble nature mourns her loss,
The spirit glories in the cross.   (pub. 1854)

It is little wonder the city of Sheffield honoured him so lavishly at his final farewell. A man for all people? His city thought so!

A demanding decade

The years 1830–1840 presented Montgomery with some of his most demanding and interesting work. The Sheffield Literary and Philosophical Society had been launched in 1822. Its purpose was, among other things, to arrange six or eight lectures each year and organize a number of social events to bring the dignitaries of the city together. Montgomery was president of the society between 1824 and 1827, and he was again elected president in 1833.

At the society's first meeting in 1833 the appointed lecturer proved to be a disappointment. As president, it fell to Montgomery to draw the lectures to a premature end and deal with the disillusioned lecturer. This proved difficult as Montgomery did not altogether share the views of his members and thought that the unfortunate lecturer was 'much like himself'.

As a now established literary figure and scholar, Montgomery continued to travel widely and to give his lectures on poetry. In the previous chapter we saw that during the 1830s, he visited London (1831); Leeds, Newcastle and Manchester (1836); Bristol (1838); and Nottingham (1839). We may think this to be a reasonable commitment, but travel then was slow and tiring and Montgomery was never blessed with robust health.

Such was his reputation as a scholar that the University of Edinburgh considered offering him the prestigious position of Professor of Rhetoric. Although Montgomery was honoured, he indicated that if the post was offered, he would decline it. Perhaps he did not see his Christian faith as compatible with a secular professorship, or maybe he just did not wish to leave Sheffield and his many friends.

In 1832 the cholera epidemic, which had seriously affected other parts of the country, particularly the north-east, arrived in Sheffield. The effect on the city was so severe that during that year nearly 450 of its citizens died. The day of 22 August 1832 was appointed 'a day of humiliation and prayer'. Never before had there been such a day in Sheffield.

Montgomery took a daily and active interest in the course of the epidemic. With the civic leaders, medical authorities and church ministers he sought to bring practical help and comfort to the sick and to relatives of those who lost their lives. As chairman of the Board of Health he had particular duties for the discipline of isolation that was essential if the epidemic was to be controlled.

Sensitive to the events that were unfolding, Montgomery gave the people two hymns to sing. We may not find them an inspiration today but they contributed to the expression of the human spirit in those dark times. The first struck a sombre note—'Let the land mourn through all its coasts'—and the second, more uplifting, began, 'It is the Lord, behold His hand', a recognition of a 'higher throne'.

When the epidemic had run its course the Cholera Monument was erected at the place where the dead had been buried. It was sited in Clay Wood, a planted and picturesque area about a mile from the centre of the

Cholera monument (from Holland and Everett, *Memoirs of James Montgomery,* vol. 5, 1856, p. 109)

city. The monument was in the form of an obelisk, and the foundation and cornerstone were laid by Montgomery. He composed a poem, 'The Cholera Mount' (dated 1832), to mark the occasion. Those who wish to read the poignant words of the poem can find them in Montgomery's *Poetical Works* (see Bibliography).

An altogether happier occasion was the coronation of Queen Victoria. Victoria, the daughter of Edward, Duke of Kent, came to the throne at the age of eighteen when her uncle King William IV died in 1837. Victoria was crowned in 1838 and she married Albert, Prince of Saxe-Coburg, in 1840. Although Sheffield could not be regarded then as a royalist city, celebrations on the day of the coronation were enthusiastic.

As a leading citizen, Montgomery was called upon to play a prominent part in the preparations for the celebrations. The summer weather of 1838 and the coronation gave the nation a reason to cheer. The youthful sovereign won the hearts of the people, and the citizens of the steel city were no exception. A large gathering was organized in the Cutlers Hall, and Montgomery was invited to preside and to prepare a suitable 'ode' to be sung by the assembled crowd. The writers of the *Memoirs* report that Montgomery was unwell on the day of the celebrations but was fortunately able to fulfil his duties, though with some difficulty. It pleased Montgomery that on this notable occasion he was seated beside his oldest female companion, Sarah Gales. On the other side was his niece, the lovely Harriet Montgomery, daughter of his brother Ignatius.

In his address to the gathering, Montgomery was not afraid to speak to the Christians of the city. He began, 'Friends, neighbours, fellow citizens, fellow Christians …' Continuing, he said,

We are gathered on holy ground, ground on which all true-hearted, high-minded Britons may hail each other as loyalists and patriots, brothers and sisters in one national family of which our maiden Queen—she who was lately the 'daughter of England'—by a happy transmigration has become the mother of millions, and worthy of all love, honour and obedience which dutiful children delight to yield to the dearest authority under heaven …

For those who wonder what James Montgomery looked like, it may be helpful to include a description of him as printed in the *New York Times* around the close of this demanding decade: 'Montgomery was of middle stature, slight and with yellow hair, rather melancholy expression of feature and accustomed to wear the lower part of his face hidden in a loose neck-cloth. His appearance was that of a clergyman of the old-school.' As to his character, throughout his life it seems that others 'esteemed him better than himself', and his sense of humour was never hidden for long. These rather charming graces were the reason for his wide appeal wherever he went.

Going home

The Lord promised his earthly disciples that he would return and take them—escort them—to his Father's house, to a place prepared for them (John 14). For James Montgomery, the Lord came to The Mount on 30 April 1854. He came to take his servant home.

Early that year, Montgomery began to complain of a stomach disorder, a problem he had endured from time to time during his life. His doctor was called, treatment was given and temporary relief came. John Holland called at The Mount on 29 April to be informed by Montgomery, 'I feel considerable discomfort here', placing his hands on his stomach. At lunchtime on the following day, friend Holland was summoned to The Mount to be gently told that Montgomery had died.

At family worship on the preceding evening, Montgomery indicated that, contrary to the usual practice, he would prefer Sarah, rather than himself, to read the Scriptures. 'You must read,' he said. He then knelt to pray, as was his custom. 'He was a bit edgy,' Sarah commented. Eventually he retired to his room. The following morning, a servant found him prostrate on the floor. He said he had been there for several hours. His doctor was called again but was unable to do anything, and Montgomery's eventful life was at an end.

The funeral service was held at St George's Church on 11 May. George Pagdin, a Sheffield writer, describes the day:

Such demonstrations of respect were never paid to any individual in Sheffield before. The shops were generally closed. Many factories and other places of business were deserted. The houses showed signs of mourning. Along the route of the procession housetops and windows and side-streets were filled with respectful spectators. Great numbers of people were around St George's Church, in the graveyard and on every elevation that commanded a view of the event.

It is fitting that Canon Emeritus Dr George Tolley, former Dean of Sheffield Cathedral, should also describe this eventful day: 'His funeral was a great public occasion. Factories, shops and offices closed. Crowds lined the streets for the hour-long cortège which included every individual and organization of note in the town … certainly nothing like it has been

Statue of James Montgomery in the grounds of Sheffield Cathedral

seen since.' It was a moving day, and one of great thankfulness, as Sheffield paid tribute to one of its greatest Christian citizens.

A man like David? Not a king, but a servant of the Lord, a man through whom God could fulfil his will (Acts 13:22).

Postscript

Little has been written about the financial affairs of Montgomery, except for reference to the purchase and sale of the newspapers with their printing machinery and the annual pension he was granted. It may be assumed that he was paid for his lectures and the sales of his poetry. It is fair to say that by careful use of his incomes he became a reasonably wealthy man.

At the time of Montgomery's death in 1854 there was no knowledge of a will. By diligent search, however, an envelope was found containing a document written in Montgomery's hand and dated 24 March 1842. This was his Last Will and Testament. It includes the following legacies to:

* the minister of the Fulneck Brethren—£300;
* the treasurer of the Moravian Brethren Missions—£300;
* the charity school for poor boys of Sheffield—£50;
* a charity school for poor girls—£50 (no favouritism!).

There follow donations to many charitable organizations, mainly of £25–£50. Then come donations to family and friends:

* John Holland—£100;
* Anne Gales—£400;
* Sarah Gales—£400.

Various items of his property were left to his brother Ignatius. Household furniture was left to the Gales sisters. Books and pictures were to be given to some of his friends, and the residue was to go to his brothers.

A number of aspects of this Last Will and Testament call for comment. Firstly, the will was made over twenty years before his death and some of the beneficiaries had died before the will was implemented. Secondly, the document was littered with later marks made by Montgomery. Thirdly, the will shows Montgomery's meticulous care in the handling of his wealth. And fourthly, his library was to be auctioned, but it was eventually housed at Fulneck.

Hymns of glory, songs of praise

1 Better than life itself, Thy love,
Dearer than all beside to me;
For whom have I in heaven above,
Or what on earth, compared with Thee!

2 Praise with all my heart, my mind, my voice,
For all Thy mercies I will give,
My soul shall still in God rejoice;
My tongue shall bless Thee while I live.

('Psalm LXIII', 1867)

Opinions vary!

In his work *A Collection of Writings on Hymnology*, Canon John Ellerton (1826–1893) wrote of Montgomery, 'He was our first hymnologist; the first Englishman who collected and criticised hymns, and who made people that had lost all recollection of ancient models understand something of what a hymn meant and what it ought to be.' High praise indeed! Ellerton was almost certainly referring to Montgomery's work *The Christian Psalmist*, with its Introductory Essay, written in 1825. There is no doubt that this was a defining piece of critical hymnology in which Montgomery assessed the works of other hymn-writers as well as his own.

John and Charles Wesley had produced the *Charlestown Collection of Psalms and Hymns* in Georgia in 1737. Newton and Cowper had collaborated to publish *Olney Hymns* in 1779. Even earlier, Isaac Watts had produced his *Hymns and Spiritual Songs* in 1707. Montgomery's little hymn collection, written at Fulneck when he was a youthful thirteen-year-old, heralded the hymn-writer of substance he was to become.

As a general and generous assessment of Montgomery's hymn-writing, Julian's *Dictionary of Hymnology* (London, 1892) can hardly be equalled, even though it is now dated:

As a hymn-writer he [Montgomery] ranks in popularity with Wesley, Watts, Doddridge, Newton and Cowper. The secrets of his power as a hymn-writer were manifold. His poetic genius was of a high order, his knowledge of Scripture was extensive, his devotional spirit was of the holiest type and his Christian views broad

90 James Montgomery: a man for all people

and charitable. With the faith of a strong man he united the beauty and simplicity of a child but bequeathed to the Church of Christ wealth which could only have come from true genius and a sanctified heart.

Josiah Conder, a perceptive hymn critic and composer, wrote in his Preface to *The Congregational Hymn Book* (1836), 'He must be a bold man ... who would attempt to improve the compositions of Mr Montgomery; but it would be absurd to feel a similar delicacy with regard to the rude and homely compositions of Hart and Cennick.' In defence of those earlier writers, it must be said that in their day they not only had written useful contributions to Christian worship, but also had been popular hymn-writers influenced by Moravian teaching and worship.

More recently, Bernard L. Manning, in his highly acclaimed work on Wesley and Watts (1942), writes, 'The more Montgomery is read the more his solid merit appears. It is a merit that is easily missed, for it has no showiness to recommend it.' Erik Routley writes, '... he is the greatest bridge between the eighteenth and nineteenth centuries in hymnody, and his style shows marks of the best, and occasionally the weakest, characteristics of both ages.' Garrett Horder, himself a respected hymnologist, expressed the view that Montgomery's hymns had 'variety, clearness, strength, suitability of form ... they have rarely, if ever, been excelled.'

James Montgomery wrote some 400 hymns, compared with the 600 given to us by Isaac Watts and probably around 6,000 by Charles Wesley. By no means all the hymns written by such prolific writers deserve to be sung in our generation. Yet the words of the very best hymns not only enhance the worship of today's church but also linger in the mind. Montgomery spoke of '... those hymns, which once heard, are remembered without effort, remembered involuntarily, yet remembered with renewed and increasing delight at every revival'. The 20th-century renewal movements have brought to the church some worthy hymns and songs for Christian voices to sing. It will be of interest to see how many remain popular and are remembered in years to come.

Hymnody is ever reinventing itself in a variety of modes. The Watts, Wesley and Montgomery hymns were written for an age now long passed and for musical accompaniments that differ from those we are familiar with today. It is a tribute to those hymn-writers that so many of their works remain a valuable part of Christian worship. When Montgomery was asked how much of his work would last, his reply was, 'None; nothing sir, except perhaps a few of my hymns'. Dr George Wiley, writing as recently as the year 2000, comments, '… Montgomery's achievement is considerable, and whilst fashions and contexts, even taste for hymns do change, a few of Montgomery's are likely to be sung as long as … Christianity itself endures.'

The Montgomery hymn collections

From his childhood days at Fulneck, Montgomery had been raised in the world of hymn-singing. The Moravian hymn-book, which was familiar to Montgomery, contained Christian convictions which fashioned his faith. Bishop Cooper writes, 'The Moravian Church gave to hymn-singing a prominence in worship not to be met in other communions.' The large Moravian settlements at Ockbrook and Fulneck had traditions of joyfully singing hymns, especially by German composers such as Gerhardt, Tersteegen and Zinzendorf. It was from these masters that Montgomery learned his craft. He wrote later in life of those days of 'singing meetings' when he 'had often lain in bed and listened with inexpressible delight to this social singing'.

Earlier he had recorded his vivid impressions: 'The hymns of the Moravians were full of ardent expressions, tender complaints, and animated prayers: these were my delight. As soon as I could spell, I had filled a little volume with sacred poems, though I was almost entirely unacquainted with our great English poets.'

Having launched himself on the absorbing work of hymn-writing, he was to use his poetic skills in the various causes of reform to which his then master, Joseph Gales, was himself committed. Even so, it seems that, for several years after leaving school, his greater interest was in the composition of poetry rather than hymns. Bishop Joseph Cooper writes, 'He usually wrote on half sheets of writing paper, at the foot of each composition were the date it was written and his signature, many were written on request for special occasions.'

In the days of Montgomery, St Paul's Church in Sheffield (now demolished) was situated in what are now the Peace Gardens adjacent to the Town Hall. In 1810, Thomas Cotterill, the vicar of St Paul's, published *A Selection of Psalms and Hymns for Public and Private Use, Adapted for the Services* of *the Church of England*. In 1819, James Montgomery rose to the challenge of assisting Cotterill in a revision of his hymn selection. This volume contained some 350 hymns, of which a number were Montgomery's own compositions. Cotterill employed Montgomery 'for his wise judgement and knowledge of what a good congregational hymn should be'. In his role as editor and publisher, Montgomery also undertook the printing of the book. The publication of this Cotterill–Montgomery collection did not, however, find favour with the congregation of St Paul's. As Dr George Tolley comments, 'We should remember that the Anglican

St Paul's Church, Sheffield; now the site of the Peace Gardens (from *St Paul's Church*, by William Odom, 1919)

tradition of hymn singing of the nineteenth century had developed against considerable opposition. Hymns were not allowed in Anglican liturgy; psalms yes, hymns no!'

The controversy was referred to the Ecclesiastical Court in York. This might seem somewhat heavy-handed from today's perspective, but it was an issue which affected the established church and needed to be clarified by canon law. In 1820, Archbishop Vernon-Harcourt in York undertook to adjudicate in the controversy and to give a judgement. Eventually, ecclesiastical approval was issued and the congregation of St Paul's settled down to a more amiable frame of mind. The new collection of *Psalms and Hymns* became popular and, despite continued opposition from the Southern See of Canterbury and the Bishop of Peterborough, it helped to mould the hymn-books of the future. It is possible that the high praise given to Montgomery by Canon Ellerton and cited at the start of this chapter was based in part on the contribution made to Anglican worship by the Cotterill hymn-book. Dr George Tolley writes, 'The "Archbishop's Collection", as the new hymn-book was known, became so popular that 29 editions were eventually published.'

By the 1820s, James Montgomery had achieved excellence in the art of hymn-writing. Perhaps by then he was at the peak of his considerable powers. He had fully recovered his personal faith and in 1825 he shed his responsibilities for publishing *The Iris*. The year 1822 saw the first major collection published by Montgomery. Its title, *Songs of Zion*, revealed its nature. It was an 'Imitation of the Psalms' containing sixty-seven versions (later to be enlarged to seventy-two) of the psalms of David. According to Dr Wiley, Montgomery's presentation of the psalms had only moderate success. The exception was the famous 'imitation' of Psalm 72, with its well-known opening line, 'Hail to the Lord's Anointed' and which is still popular today. Bishop Joseph Cooper writes, 'Although *Songs of Zion* cost Montgomery a large amount of labour, like others ... he did not find it easy to keep the full meaning of the original text, and at the same time produce good poetry in modern language.' Montgomery recognized the difficulty he and others faced. He notes, 'It is far from popular to become the champion of the cross, even in this way, but it must be an honour to any poet to furnish words in which sincere Christians may express their joys and their sorrows, their hopes and their fears, and to do this has been my design in these Imitations of the Psalms.'

Then came *The Christian Psalmist*, published in 1825. It carried the subtitle *Hymns Original and Selected*, indicating that the works of other writers were included. The volume as published contained 562 hymns, of which 103 were by Montgomery. Montgomery complemented his own work by perceptive, penetrating and gentle comments on the writing of hymns. He wrote a long Introductory Essay which was then regarded as a classic appraisal of his own works, a valuable guide to his mind and a commentary on the works of other writers. Today's readers would find it a useful guide to hymnody. Here is an extract, in which Montgomery describes in typical detail what he regarded as some principles required for good hymn-writing:

A hymn ought to be as regular in its structure as any other poem; it should have a distinct subject, and that subject should be simple, not complicated, so that whatever skill or labour might be required in the author to develop his plan, there should be little or none required on the part of the reader to understand it. Consequently, a hymn should have a beginning, middle, and end. There should be a manifest graduation in the thoughts, and their mutual dependence should be so perceptible, that they could not be transposed without injuring the unity of the piece; every line carrying forward the connection and every verse adding a well-proportioned limb to a symmetrical body. The reader should know when the strain is complete, and be satisfied, as at the close of an air in music; while defects and superfluities should be felt by him as annoyances, in whatsoever part they might occur.

He makes comments in the same essay, usually gently but sometimes forcefully, about the works of others. 'Hymns ... appear to have been written by all kinds of people except poets; and why ... is obvious. Just in proportion as the religion of Christ is understood and taught in primitive purity, those who either believe not its spirituality or who have not proved its converting influence, are careful to avoid meddling with it ...' Later he writes, 'Many of our eminent poets ... either knew not, or contemned, "the truth as it is in Jesus".'

Unlike his contemporary Josiah Conder, Montgomery held many of his predecessors in high regard. Of Isaac Watts he could write, 'He has, with his usual accuracy, embraced a compass and variety of subjects, which include and illustrate every truth of revelation … whether of sin, nature, or grace, and describes every trial, temptation, conflict, doubt, fear, and grief; as well as the faith, hope, charity, love, joy, peace, labour, and patience of the Christian'; a generous tribute from such a reputable writer to the even more illustrious Watts. It was the genuine godliness of Watts as a hymn-writer that appealed to Montgomery. He writes about 'the piety of Watts, the ardour of Wesley and the tenderness of Doddridge'.

Montgomery admired variety in hymn composition and referred to this attribute in the hymns of Charles Wesley. As usual, Montgomery is precise and perceptive, writing, 'Christian experience furnishes him [Wesley] with everlasting and inexhaustible themes, and … he has celebrated them with an affluence of diction, and splendour of colouring, rarely surpassed'.

He had a similar regard for the work of the evangelical Anglican Augustus Toplady, who, having had some contact with early Methodism, opposed Wesley's Arminianism from a position of vigorous Calvinism. Some of Toplady's hymns have a peculiarly ethereal spirit, which appealed to Montgomery. He writes, 'whether mourning or rejoicing, praying or praising, the writer seems absorbed in the full triumph of faith, and whether in the body or out of the body, caught up into the third heaven, and beholding unutterable things.'

Montgomery adds a salutary warning to fellow hymn-writers: 'authors who devote their talents to the glory of God and the salvation of men, ought surely to take as much pains to polish and perfect their offerings as secular poets bestow on their works.' Any reader who wishes to follow the history and appreciate the art of hymn-writing should be aware of this classic commentary on hymnology in this Introductory Essay to *The Christian Psalmist*.

Montgomery was an ardent admirer of the hymns of John Newton of Olney. An early Protestant hymn-book, *Olney Hymns*, had been published in 1779, the year of Montgomery's birth. *Olney Hymns* had a collection of over 300 hymns. It first appeared in three volumes: *On Selected Texts of Scripture*; *On Occasional Subjects*; and *On the Progress and Changes in the Spiritual Life*. Of the published hymns, 68 were by William Cowper and some 280 by John Newton. *Olney Hymns* passed through several editions, and in 1829, two decades after Newton's death, Montgomery undertook to write an Introductory Essay to *Olney Hymns* republished that year. He wrote of the hymn-book, 'It ought to be forever dear to the Christian public as an unprecedented memorial … of the power of divine grace.' Cowper's hymns were often expressions of his own personal devotions, periods of sadness and trials of faith. They appealed strongly to Montgomery, who could identify in some measure with the emotional turmoil which often afflicted the Olney poet. The pathos of Cowper's personality was not matched to the same degree in the make-up of the Sheffield poet, but Montgomery did understand something of Cowper's nervous temperament. Indeed, in Montgomery's view, only William Cowper could be considered a consistently great poet, a 'Mighty Master'. He did, however, give Isaac Watts the accolade 'The greatest name among hymn-writers'. Those who value highly the hymns of Charles Wesley will be interested to know that he ranked a lowly third! Of course, that was only Montgomery's view!

John Newton was a prolific writer unaffected by the temperamental changes in mood that affected his Olney friend. Newton was more extrovert and was conscious of the needs of those less fortunate than himself. He was a writer whose hymns focused sharply on the essential features of the Christ-centred faith. It is not difficult to see why Montgomery had such an enthusiasm for the Olney poets; they were expressing those fundamental truths of the gospel that he himself had embraced. The compilers of Montgomery's *Memoirs* express the view that the Introductory Essay to *Olney Hymns* was Montgomery's most successful piece of writing, yet it never achieved the fame of the essay introducing *The Christian Psalmist*.

By 1835, Montgomery's standing with the Moravian Brethren was so high that he was commissioned to undertake a revision of the Moravian hymn-book containing over 1,000 hymns. This was a massive undertaking for a man in his mid-sixties. After nearly a decade of intermittent work on the revision he wrote to a member of the Provincial Elders Conference,

I have made many hundred memoranda in pencil, but the more I entered into the work, the more the difficulties of producing anything likely to be satisfactory, either to myself or our congregations, pressed upon my mind ... I became so discouraged that during two years past I have scarcely returned to the work for more than a few minutes at a time ...

I intend, during the coming winter, to consider what may be done towards rendering some portions of the hymns readable and ... acceptable to competent judges ... and with our Saviour's blessing.

He worked until he reached hymn 48, by which time he recorded his exasperation: 'It is the misfortune of the Brethren's Psalmody, that the ears of the congregation are *permitted* [permeated?] by mean verbiage and flat jangling of terminology, which are quite as bad in poetry as false notes are in music. Every page of this volume exemplifies these inaccuracies, to call them by no harder name. Why are the praises of God not to be sung to the most harmonious strains?' Although Montgomery had always been enthusiastic for the worship hymns of the Moravian Brethren, they were clearly not without flaws when viewed with the critical eye of a poet who sought perfection.

The revision undertaken by Montgomery was presented in three volumes of notes to the committee appointed by the 1847 synod and was sanctioned for use by the General Synod held in Herrnhut in 1848.

The Moravian authorities, however, added some of their own choices and discarded others. By 1874 the new hymn-book edited by Montgomery had been in use for twenty-five years but, despite all Montgomery's labours, little of his work was actually used. The writer of *The Development of the Moravian Hymn-Book* offers the interesting view expressed in 'The Messenger', a Moravian magazine, that 'a great many more of Montgomery's very fine hymns were to be found in the hymn-books of other churches than his own Moravian hymnal'.

In 1853, only a year before his death (or 'promotion to glory', as General Booth of the Salvation Army would later have said), Montgomery published what was perhaps his most important collection of hymns. He chose the title *Original Hymns for Public, Private and Social Devotion*. This hymn-book contained 355 of his hymns, almost a complete collection of his own hymn-writing. He had been working on the volume for several years, afraid that if he delayed there would be disappointment for his friends and for an expectant public. John Holland, realizing the urgency and the poet's declining energies, agreed to take Montgomery's manuscript and to complete the work for publication. He collected the valuable bundle of papers from Montgomery, writing, 'I … marched off with the precious deposit, a bundle of ominous bulk, under my arm and with the parting admonition, to beware I was not robbed!' Eventually Montgomery expressed his entire satisfaction with the final version of his last work.

Selected hymns

The hymns of James Montgomery may have declined in popularity in recent years but in traditional hymn-books there remains an encouraging selection of his work. The Anglican *Hymns Ancient and Modern* (Revised, 1950) has ten Montgomery hymns; the Moravian *Hymn-Book and Liturgy* (1969) has thirty; the Moravian Church hymn-book being prepared at the time of writing is likely to have fourteen; *Congregational Praise* (1956), which is dominated by Watts' hymns, nevertheless contains fifteen by Montgomery. *Christian Hymns* (2nd edn., 1985) has an admirable selection of twenty-six Montgomery compositions, as does the latest edition published in 2004. *The Methodist Hymn-Book and Offices* (1933) contains fourteen and *The Methodist Hymn-Book and Psalms* (1983) has only one fewer.

The classification of Montgomery's hymns by subject is difficult because, despite his own advice that hymns should have a structured unity, many of his general hymns include a variety of subjects. For the purposes of this brief commentary on some of Montgomery's hymns we will view them in three main groups: the life of Christ; the life of the Christian; and the life of the church.

The life of Christ

Two Christmas hymns on the theme of Christ's incarnation are well known. 'Angels from the Realms of Glory', perhaps one of Montgomery's finest hymns, has reference to various voices: angels from heaven, shepherds from the fields, wise men from afar, and saints before the altar; all encourage the singer to worship Christ, the newborn King. Not quite so well known but still to be found in a number of hymn collections are these verses simply entitled, 'Christmas':

1 Bright and joyful is the morn,
For to us a Child is born;
From the highest realms of heaven,
Unto us a Son is given ...

2 Wonderful in counsel He:
The Incarnate Deity,
Sire of ages ne'er to cease,
King of kings, and Prince of peace.

3 Come and worship at His feet,
Yield to Christ the homage meet,
From His manger to His throne,
Homage due to God alone.

The Moravian influence inspired Montgomery to write often about the death of Christ. His most famous hymn on the theme of Christ's redemptive suffering begins, 'Go to dark Gethsemane ...' words which set the scene for what is a narrative hymn. Here is the whole hymn, taking the singer with the Lord from the turmoil of the garden to the triumph of the resurrection:

1 Go to dark Gethsemane,
Ye that feel the tempter's power,
Your Redeemer's conflict see:
Watch with Him one bitter hour.
Turn not from His griefs away;
Learn of Jesus Christ to pray.

2 Follow to the judgement-hall;
View the Lord of life arraigned.
Oh, the wormwood and the gall!
Oh, the pangs His soul sustained!
Shun not suffering, shame or loss:
Learn of Him to bear the cross.

3 Calvary's mournful mountain climb;
There, adoring at His feet,
Mark that miracle of time,
God's own sacrifice complete.
'It is finished,' hear Him cry:
Learn of Jesus Christ to die.

4 Early hasten to the tomb,
Where they laid His breathless clay.
All is solitude and gloom:
Who hath taken Him away?
Christ is risen;—He seeks the skies.
Saviour, teach us so to rise.

An unfamiliar hymn on the theme of Christ's redeeming work is written in the form of an invitation to partake of the Saviour's offer of free remission from the 'leprosy of sin'. Selected verses follow:

1 Come to Calvary's holy mountain,
Sinners ruined by the fall;
Here a pure and healing fountain
Flows to you, to me, to all,
In a full perpetual tide,—
Opened when the Saviour died …

2 Come in sorrow and contrition,
Wounded, impotent and blind,
Here the guilty free remission,
Here the troubled peace may find;
Health this fountain will restore,
He that drinks shall thirst no more.

3 He that drinks shall live for ever;
'Tis a soul-renewing flood:
God is faithful;—God will never
Break His covenant in blood;
Signed when our redeemer died,
Sealed when he was glorified.

Montgomery's hymns reflect the Moravian emphasis on the atoning death of Christ in the biblical language of the Lamb of God and the blood of Christ (1 Peter 1:19; Eph. 1:7). In this he was influenced and inspired by Count Zinzendorf's hymns, in particular, 'Jesus, Thy blood and righteousness / My beauty are, my glorious dress'. But Montgomery never allowed his work to emulate the more bizarre expressions used by some of the Moravian writers. He was always clear but never eccentric. His reference to the 'atoning blood' was always restrained. Here is an example of Montgomery's references to the sacrifice of Christ in a hymn written for a communion service. It is reproduced in full for meditation.

1 Communion of my Saviour's blood,
In Him to have my lot and part;
To prove the virtue of that flood
Which burst on Calvary from His heart.

2 To feed by faith on Christ the bread,
His body broken on the tree;
To live in Him my living head,
Who died and rose again for me.

3 This be my joy and comfort here,
This pledge of future glory mine,
Jesus, in spirit now appear,
And break the bread and pour the wine.

4 From Thy dear hand may I receive
The tokens of Thy dying love;
And while I feast on earth, believe
That I shall feast with Thee above.

5 Ah! there, though in the lowest place,
Thee at Thy table could I meet,
And see Thee, know Thee, face to face,
For such a moment death were sweet.

6 What then will their fruition be,
Who meet in heaven with blest accord?
A moment?—No: eternity!
They are for ever with the Lord.

The last verse of the hymn 'Go to Dark Gethsemane' is a comparatively rare reference to the resurrection and ascension of the Lord Jesus Christ. But Christ's triumph over death, a vital element in the apostolic gospel, is also found elsewhere; for example, in a hymn entitled 'The God of Providence and Grace', the last verse of which is also a plea for full consecration:

On Him who bore Thy chastening rod,
That we might by His stripes be healed;
He died for us—the Lamb of God!
He rose—and our redemption sealed.
And shall we, dare we, can we still
Resist Thy fear, Thy love despise?
No, take us, soul, affection, will,
A free and living sacrifice.

One event in the life of Jesus which evidently captured the mind and heart of Montgomery was the pageant of the entry of the King into Jerusalem (Matt. 21). He wrote several hymns on this theme. Here he writes for children:

1 When Jesus into Salem rode,
The children sang around;
For joy they plucked their palms and strowed
Their garments on the ground.

2 Hosanna, our glad voices raise,
Hosanna to our King;
Should we forget our Saviour's praise
The stones themselves would sing.

One of the most famous and popular hymns that Montgomery wrote, one which appears in almost every well-known collection of hymns, is 'Hail to the Lord's Anointed'. It is an adoration of Christ and his earthly work. Montgomery found his inspiration for this fine hymn in Psalm 72, but discerning readers will find echoes of the 'Nazareth manifesto' recorded by Luke (Luke 4:18–19).

Verses are presented in different orders in different publications. The order preferred by Montgomery is as follows:

1 Hail to the Lord's Anointed!
Great David's greater Son!
Hail, in the time appointed,
His reign on earth begun!
He comes to break oppression,
To set the captive free,
To take away transgression,
And rule in equity.

2 He shall come down like showers
Upon the fruitful earth;
And love, joy, hope, like flowers,
Spring in His path to birth.
Before Him, on the mountains,
Shall peace, the herald, go;
And righteousness, in fountains,
From hill to valley flow.

3 Arabia's desert-ranger
To Him shall bow the knee;
The Ethiopian stranger
His glory come to see;
With offerings of devotion,
Ships from the isles shall meet,
To pour the wealth of ocean
In tribute at His feet.

4 Kings shall fall down before Him,
And gold and incense bring;
All nations shall adore Him,
His praise all people sing:
For He shall have dominion
O'er river, sea and shore,
Far as the eagle's pinion
Or dove's light wing can soar.

5 For Him shall prayer unceasing
And daily vows ascend;
His kingdom still increasing,—
A kingdom without end.
The mountain-dew shall nourish
A seed in weakness sown,
Whose fruit shall spread and flourish,
And shake like Lebanon.

6 O'er every foe victorious,
He on His throne shall rest;
From age to age more glorious,
All blessing and all blessed.
The tide of time shall never
His covenant remove:
His name shall stand for ever:
That name to us is—Love.

If this was Montgomery's order, as published in his *Poetical Works* (1867), it has been varied in *The Moravian Hymn Book* by the insertion of the following verse (at v. 2) from a hymn entitled 'Christ's Reign':

Chapter 6

He comes, with succour speedy,
To all who suffer wrong:
To help the poor and needy,
And bid the week be strong;
To give them songs for sighing,
Their darkness turn to light,
Whose souls, in bondage lying,
Were precious in His sight.

The insertion occurs also in *The Methodist Hymn-Book* (1933) and *Hymns Ancient and Modern* (Revised, 1950). For a number of commentators on the hymns of Montgomery—for example, Faith Cook—this well-known hymn takes pride of place among his psalm renderings.

The life of the Christian

True to his evangelical persuasions, Montgomery did not avoid the reality and unpleasantness of human sin. He stressed its universality. For Montgomery, the gospel was God's covenant plan for the cleansing of the human heart from its defilement. He wrote 'The World Lost and Redeemed', in which he deals with the consequences of sin and the triumph of redemption for sinners through Christ:

The world in condemnation lay;
And death from Adam reigning
O'er man maintained remorseless sway;
While sin, his soul enchaining,
Foredoomed the second death to all,
That shared the ruin of the fall,
But Christ's triumphant mission
Redeemed us from perdition ...

Should there be any doubt about Montgomery's biblical orthodoxy on the matter of the human predicament, this is what he pens at a personal level:

Lord, when we search the human heart,
We find a fallen world within;
There is no health in any part;
Sin reigns throughout, and death by sin.

Although this hymn fails to point to the remedy as clearly as it might do, it does include the lines,

The smallest portion of the whole
… Some beams of heavenly truth pervade;
Slowly the day-spring o'er the soul
Breaks through the fog of nature's shade.

There is happy release, redemption and reconciling grace for all who acknowledge their sin and trust in the Saviour. For Montgomery, God was full of grace and mercy. The following hymn demonstrates how he expressed the human response of repentance and faith to divine mercy. Entitled 'Repentance', the hymn turns the singer helpfully to Jesus, the only Saviour.

1 Mercy alone can meet my case;
For mercy, Lord, I cry,
Jesus, Redeemer, show Thy face
In mercy, or I die …

2 To this, this only will I cleave,
Thy word is all my plea;
That word is truth, and I believe:—
Have mercy, Lord, on me.

The Christian life, entered through faith, is a journey fraught with temptations and danger. Yet Montgomery can encourage the Christian pilgrim to rely on the Lord for strength upon strength for the warfare. This next psalm-hymn is inspired by the words of David, 'The LORD is my light and my salvation; Whom shall I fear?' (Ps. 27:1). It is worth tracing the words of David through this short work of Montgomery's. It appears in some well-known hymn collections.

1 God is my strong salvation,
What foe have I to fear?

In darkness and temptation,
My light, my help is near:

2 Though hosts may camp around me,
Firm in the fight I stand;
What terror can confound me
With God at my right hand?

3 Place on the Lord reliance;
My soul, with courage wait;
His truth be thine affiance,
When faint and desolate …

4 His might thy heart shall strengthen,
His love thy joy increase;
Mercy thy days shall lengthen;
The Lord will give thee peace.

It could be said that, above all, James Montgomery was a man of prayer. Each day saw him at the throne of heavenly grace. Faith Cook writes, 'Meditation on the believer's communion with God, as he seeks his face in prayer, is expressed in some of the poet's enduring lines.' J. R. Watson describes Montgomery's hymn which begins 'O Thou by Whom we Come to God' as 'the greatest of all hymns on the difficult subject of prayer'. Watson goes on helpfully, 'He understands that it [prayer] is central to the Christian life and that without prayer Christian discipleship lapses into moral behaviour.' For Montgomery, prayer is no light-hearted reciting of formal prayers, nor is it an easy-going approach to an undemanding God. Prayer is a serious discipline as well as a delight of the redeemed life. Without further comment, here are two of Montgomery's best-known eight-verse hymns on prayer for comparison and contemplation.

1 LORD, teach us how to pray aright,
With reverence and with fear;
Though dust and ashes in Thy sight,
We may, we must draw near.

2 We perish if we cease from prayer;
O grant us power to pray!
And when to meet Thee we prepare,
O meet us by the way.

3 Burdened with guilt, convinced of sin,
In weakness, want and woe,
Fightings without, and fear within;
Lord, whither shall we go?

4 God of all grace, we come to Thee
With broken, contrite hearts;
Give what Thine eye delights to see,
Truth in the inward parts.

5 Give deep humility; the sense
Of godly sorrow give;
A strong, desiring confidence
To hear Thy voice and live.

6 Faith in the only sacrifice
That can for sin atone;
To cast our hopes, to fix our eyes,
On Christ, on Christ alone.

7 Patience to watch and wait and weep,
Though mercy long delay;
Courage, our fainting souls to keep,
And trust Thee though Thou slay.

8 Give these, and then Thy will be done;
Thus strengthened with Thy might,
We by Thy Spirit and Thy Son
Shall pray, and pray aright.

1 O Thou by whom we come to God,
The Life, the Truth, the Way,
The path of prayer Thyself hast trod;
Lord, *teach* us how to pray.

2 Prayer is the soul's sincere desire,
Uttered or unexpressed;
The motion of a hidden fire
That trembles in the breast:

3 Prayer is the burden of a sigh,
The falling of a tear;
The upward glancing of an eye
When none but God is near.

4 Prayer is the simplest form of speech
That infant lips can try;
Prayer the sublimest strains that reach
The Majesty on high:

5 Prayer is the contrite sinner's voice
Returning from his ways,
While angels in their songs rejoice,
And cry, 'Behold, he prays!'

6 Prayer is the Christian's vital breath,
The Christian's native air;
His watchword at the gates of death,
He enters heaven with prayer.

7 Nor prayer is made on earth alone:
The Holy Spirit pleads;
And Jesus, on the eternal throne,
For sinners intercedes.

8 O Thou by whom we come to God,
The Life, the Truth, the Way,
The path of prayer Thyself hast trod;
Lord, *teach* us how to pray.

These two great hymns, which have been an inspiration to those who seek to pray and pray aright, by no means exhaust Montgomery's contribution to the subject of prayer. The prayer given by the Lord Jesus Christ as instruction and inspiration to his disciples (Matt. 6; Luke 11) is paraphrased in this next hymn, which deserves to be sung more often than is the case. It was written in 1825.

1 Our heavenly Father, hear
The prayer we offer now;
Thy name be hallowed far and near,
To Thee all nations bow.

2 Thy kingdom come; Thy will
On earth be done in love.
As saints and seraphim fulfill
The perfect law above.

3 Our daily bread supply,
While by Thy word we live.
The guilt of our iniquity
Forgive as we forgive.

4 From dark temptation's power,
From Satan's wiles defend;
Deliver in the evil hour,
And guide us to the end.

5 Thine, then, forever be
Glory and power divine;
The sceptre, throne and majesty
Of heaven and earth be Thine.

A high priority of the Christian life for Montgomery was personal holiness reflecting, though imperfectly, the holiness of God. The agent of holiness in the Christian is the Holy Spirit indwelling, inspiring and enabling the Christian to live a holy life. Hymns on holiness in the Montgomery corpus are not difficult to find; a comparatively large number are found in hymn-books in use today. Montgomery believed that sanctification and the fullness of salvation ought to be the desire of every Christian.

1 Jesus, our best beloved Friend,
Draw out our souls in pure desire;
Jesus, in love to us descend,
Baptize us with Thy Spirit's fire.

2 On Thy redeeming name we call,
Poor and unworthy though we be;
Pardon and sanctify us all:
Let each Thy full salvation see ...

The following is a congregational hymn on the work of the Holy Spirit which is a petition for a re-enactment of the day of Pentecost. It is a popular hymn, although many a congregation would be astonished if the petition was answered in its full intent! Because Montgomery lived in the afterglow of the 18th-century revival, his writing expresses discernable desires for a new work of the Spirit in his own life and times.

1 LORD God, the Holy Ghost,
In this accepted hour,
On this the day of Pentecost,
Descend in all Thy power;
We meet, with one accord,
In this Thy Holy place,
And wait the promise of our Lord—
The Spirit of all grace.

2 Like mighty rushing wind
Upon the waves beneath,
Move with one impulse every mind,
One soul, one feeling breathe—
The young, the old, inspire
With wisdom from above;
And give us hearts and tongues of fire,
To pray and praise and love.

3 Spirit of light! explore
And chase our gloom away
With lustre shining more and more
Unto the perfect day:
Spirit of Truth! be Thou
In life and death our guide;
Spirit of adoption! *now*
May we be sanctified!

Through many toils and joys, Bunyan's pilgrim finds his way to the Celestial City. That is the hope of every Christian on his or her journey of life. Earth is but a temporary dwelling. The Father's house is the Christian's permanent home (John 14). 'Earth is our lodge and heaven is our home,' wrote Isaac Watts. This heavenly theme occupied much of Montgomery's hours of meditation and found its way into some of his very best verses. Here is a little-known work entitled 'Preparation for Heaven'. It will be seen that holiness and heaven are inextricably joined.

1 Heaven is a place of rest from sin;
But all who hope to enter there,
Must here that holy course begin,
Which shall their souls for rest prepare.

2 Clean hearts, O GOD in us create;
Right spirits, LORD, in us renew;
Commence we now that higher state,
Now do Thy will as angels do.

3 A life in heaven!—Oh, what is this?—
The sum of all that faith believed,
Fulness of joy and depths of bliss,
Unseen, unfathomed, unconceived ...

4 Firm in His footsteps may we tread,
Learn every lesson of His love,
And be from glory to glory led,
From heaven below to heaven above.

For some, the best of all Montgomery's hymns, containing some of the highest poetry he was inspired to write, is this hymn of heaven:

1 For ever with the Lord!
Amen, so let it be;
Life from the dead is in that word;
'Tis immortality.

2 Here in the body pent,
Absent from Him I roam;
Yet nightly pitch my moving tent,
A day's march nearer home.

3 My Father's house on high,
Home of my soul, how near!
At times to faith's foreseeing eye
Thy golden gates appear.

4 My thirsty spirit faints
To reach the land I love,
The bright inheritance of saints,
Jerusalem above ...

5 For ever with the Lord!
Father, if 'tis Thy will,
The promise of that faithful word,
E'en here to me fulfil.

6 So when my latest breath
Shall rend the veil in twain,
By death I shall escape from death,
And life eternal gain.

7 Knowing as I am known,
How shall I love that word;
And oft repeat before the throne,
For ever with the Lord!

The life of the church

It is true to say that, with some exceptions, Montgomery's most influential and lasting works were his hymns for public worship. Certainly he wrote fine hymns for private devotion, as we have seen. He was powerful when writing on the themes of salvation and prayer. But he was often at his best when looking upwards rather than inwards. He used personal pronouns sparingly and carefully, avoiding mere sentimentality. His best hymns draw the singer upwards in order to be encouraged at a personal level. Martin Luther, commenting on Galatians 2:20, wrote that the heart of religion is in the personal pronouns. Montgomery would have understood what W. E. Sangster meant when he too said that the power of the gospel is in the personal pronouns. To say 'God loves you' is the word of the evangelist. To say 'God loves me' is the word of personal testimony. The students and singers of Montgomery's hymns will discover that one of his strengths is a congregational and God-ward perspective which is, at the same time, individually enlightening and encouraging. So he writes, 'LORD, teach *us* how to pray', and 'I' and 'you' are included! He gives us to sing, 'Stand up, and bless the Lord, *ye people* his choice...', and again, 'Command Thy blessings from above, / Oh God! on *all* assembled here, / Behold *us* with the Father's love, / While *we* look up with filial fear'.

Montgomery is concerned to direct attention towards and to celebrate the God who is on the high throne of heavenly sovereignty:

Hark! the song of jubilee,
Loud as mighty thunders' roar:
Of the fullness of the sea,
When it breaks upon the shore.
Hallelujah! For the LORD
God Omnipotent shall reign:
Hallelujah! Let the word
Echo round the earth and main.

There is however, a careful balance in Montgomery's work. He could extol the honour of the God who is high and lofty and who inhabits eternity, but he could also help the singer to express love for the God of covenant grace who has come to the rescue of sinners. Such grace allows the singer to enter the courts of heaven. Here is the poet in an unfamiliar psalm-song based on Psalm 116. It is suitable for both private devotion and public worship.

1 I love the Lord; He lent an ear
When I for help implored:
He rescued me from all my fear;
Therefore I love the Lord ...

2 Thou God of covenanted grace,
Hear, and record my vow,
While in Thy courts I seek Thy face,
And at Thine altar bow;

3 Henceforth to Thee myself I give,
With single heart and eye,
To walk before Thee while I live,
And bless Thee when I die.

The following is a selection of hymns, some well-known, others perhaps unfamiliar, which illustrate the high view of the Lord of Hosts which Montgomery held and which he desired his singers to appreciate. This first hymn is simply entitled 'Sabbath Worship':

1 Thousands, O Lord of Hosts! This day,
Around Thine altar meet;
And tens of thousands throng to pay
Their homage at Thy feet.

2 They see thy power and glory there,
As I have seen them too;
They read, they hear, they join in prayer,
As I am wont to do ...

3 For Thou art in their midst to teach,
When on Thy name we call;
And Thou hast blessings, Lord, for each,
Hast blessings, Lord, for all ...

4 To faith reveal the things unseen;
To hope, the joys unfold:
Let love, without a veil between,
Thy glory now behold.

5 Oh, make Thy face on me to shine,
That doubt and fear may cease;
Lift up Thy countenance benign
On me,—and give me peace.

Montgomery was never sentimental about God's ways with man. He is the Sovereign Lord over his people. Yet he is also a God of infinite grace and love. In the mystery of his person he was high and lifted up, and for Isaiah, he was 'Holy, holy, holy ... the LORD of hosts; the whole earth is full of His glory!' (Isa. 6:3). The following hymn, 'Glory to God', is a creation hymn, a Trinitarian hymn, and, at the end, a heavenly hymn! It is not chosen here to illustrate Montgomery's poetic talent (there are better hymns for that purpose), but to convey the truth that he had come to hold dear.

1 Holy, holy, holy Lord!
God of Hosts, when heaven and earth
Out of darkness, at Thy word,
Issued into glorious birth;
All Thy works around Thee stood,
And Thine eye beheld them good,
While they sang with sweet accord,
Holy, holy, holy Lord!

2 Holy, holy, holy!—Thee,
One Jehovah evermore,
Father, Son and Spirit, we,
Dust and ashes, would adore.
Lightly by the world esteemed,
From that world by Thee redeemed,
Sing we here with glad accord,
Holy, holy, holy Lord!

3 Holy, holy, holy!—All
Heaven's triumphant choir shall sing.
While the ransomed nations fall
At the footstool of the King:
Then shall saints and seraphim,
Harps and voices swell one hymn
Blending in sublime accord,
Holy, holy, holy Lord.

James Montgomery had the heart of a missionary-evangelist, with a passion for the salvation of his contemporaries. He never lost the memory of his missionary parents, who had given their lives for the evangelization of the West Indians. Montgomery's missionary hymns pulsate with a love for people and a longing for them to come to God. If evangelism was an urgent priority for Montgomery, it should also be so for the congregations that sing his verses. The following are two hymns which catch the poet's zeal for the spread of the gospel throughout the world.

1 'Let there be light'—thus spake the Word;
The Word was God;—'and there was light:'
Still the creative voice is heard;
A day is born from every night;
And every night shall turn to day,
While months, and years, and ages roll:
But we have seen a brighter ray
Dawn on the Chaos of the soul ...

2 From day to day, before our eyes,
Glows and extends the work begun:
When shall the new creation rise,
O'er every land beneath the sun?
When, in the Sabbath of his love,
Shall God from all His labours rest,
And, bending from the throne above,
Again pronounce his creatures blest!

3 As sang the morning stars of old,
Shouted the sons of God with joy;
His widening reign while we behold,
Let praise and prayer our tongues employ:
Till the redeemed, in every clime,
Yea all that breathe, and move and live,
To Christ, through every age of time,
The kingdom, power, and glory give.

The compilers of *Christian Hymns* (1977) have put the worshipping church in their debt by including the hymn 'Lift up your heads' in the section 'Worldwide Mission'. It has a militant note which would have pleased General Booth of the Salvation Army. Although it is biblical, some in today's liberal world may not be comfortable with it.

1 Lift up your heads, ye gates of brass,
Ye bars of iron yield,
And let the King of glory pass;
The cross is in the field.

2 Ye armies of the living God,
His dedicated host,
Where hallowed footsteps never trod
Take your appointed post.

3 Follow the cross; the ark of peace
Accompany your path;
To slaves and rebels bring release
From bondage and from wrath.

4 Though few and small and weak your bands,
Strong in your Captain's strength,
Go to the conquest of all lands;
All must be His at length.

5 Then fear not, faint not, halt not now
Quit you like men, be strong;
To Christ shall all the nations bow,
And sing the triumph-song.

6 Uplifted are the gates of brass,
The bars of iron yield;
Behold the King of glory pass:
The cross has won the field.

The three main ecclesiastical influences in the life of James Montgomery—the Moravians, the Methodists and the Anglicans—had a liturgical pattern of worship. The Moravian style of worship owed its inspiration to the Reformers and the *Book of Common Prayer*, which formed the basis for Anglican worship. The early Methodists were encouraged by their founders to attend the 'means of grace' in the local Anglican church as often as possible. The Lord's Supper, focusing on the death of Christ, was prominent in each tradition. Montgomery wrote several well-known hymns for that service. *The Moravian Hymn Book and Liturgy* (1960) has three Montgomery hymns in the section for the Lord's Supper. The two hymns below represent the most popular of the Montgomery hymns for the occasion of that sacrament. They properly contain strong references to the elements of the body and blood of Christ without any hint of a transubstantial interpretation. Many readers will be familiar with the words below.

1 According to Thy gracious word,
In meek humility,
This will I do, my dying Lord;
I will remember Thee.

2 Thy body, broken for my sake,
My bread from heaven shall be;
Thy testamental cup I take,
And thus remember Thee.

3 Then to the cross I turn mine eyes,
And rest on Calvary,
O Lamb of God, my sacrifice,
I must remember Thee.

4 Remember Thee, and all Thy pains,
And all Thy love to me!
Yea! While a breath, a pulse remains,
Will I remember Thee.

5 And when these failing lips grow dumb,
And mind and memory flee,
When Thou shalt in Thy kingdom come,
Then Lord, remember me.

A brief two-verse hymn is perhaps even more familiar. A third verse has been added in some hymn-books.

1 Be known to us in breaking bread,
But do not then depart;
Saviour, abide with us, and spread
Thy table in our hearts.

2 There sup with us in love divine;
Thy body and Thy blood,
That living bread, that heavenly wine,
Be our immortal food.

Montgomery valued those occasions when he could meet in the harmony of worship with his fellow Christians, and his writings contain many fine examples of 'fellowship' hymns. This chapter therefore closes with two hymns of worship and fellowship. The first, as well as being a worship hymn, also proclaims the doctrine of the Trinity and is framed in the words of congregational prayer. It is entitled 'For God's Blessing on His Assembled People':

1 Command Thy blessing from above,
O God! on all assembled here,
Behold us with a Father's love,
While we look up with filial fear.

2 Command Thy blessing, JESUS, LORD!
May we Thy true disciples be;
Speak to each heart the mighty word,
Say to the weakest, Follow me.

3 Command Thy blessings in this hour,
Spirit of Truth! and fill this place,
With humble and exalting power,
With quickening and confirming grace.

4 O Thou, our Maker, Saviour, Guide!
One true eternal God confest;
May nought in life or death divide
The saints in Thy communion blest.

5 With Thee and these for ever bound,
May all who here in prayer unite,
With harps and songs Thy throne surround,
Rest in Thy love, and reign in light.

The final work in this selection is one of Montgomery's finest and most popular hymns for congregational worship:

1 Stand up and bless the Lord,
Ye people of His choice;
Stand up and bless the Lord your God,
With heart, and soul and voice.

2 Though high above all praise,
Above all blessings high,
Who would not fear His holy name,
And laud and magnify?

3 Oh, for the living flame
From His own altar brought,
To touch our lips, our minds inspire,
And wing to heaven our thought!

4 There, with benign regard,
Our hymns He deigns to hear
Though unrevealed to mortal sense,
The spirit feels Him near.

5 God is our strength and song,
And His salvation ours;
Then be His love in Christ proclaimed
With all our ransomed powers.

6 Stand up and bless the Lord,
The Lord your God adore;
Stand up and bless His glorious name,
Henceforth for evermore.

If we allow the Bard of Sheffield to have the final word on his own hymn-writing—and we should—this is what he writes at the end of his famous *The Christian Psalmist*. After a survey of the poets and hymn-writers of his own times, he concludes,

If he who writes these sentiments knows his own heart, even if it has often deceived him, he would rather be the anonymous author of a few hymns which would become the imperishable inheritance of the people of God, than bequeath to the world another epic in the way of Homer, Virgil or our greater Milton [adapted].

The Bard of Sheffield: The longer poems

This appendix has been prepared with significant and valuable help from Dr George Wiley of Sheffield, whose book *The Poems of James Montgomery* is a critical introduction to the poet's work. It is invaluable for any reader who wishes to study more widely the poetical works of the Bard of Sheffield. (Details of Dr Wiley's book may be found in the Bibliography at the end of this book.)

W hat Dr Wiley calls 'The Longer Poems' are presented by Montgomery at the beginning of his own *Poetical Works*. It was largely on these five major poems that Montgomery won his fame as a poet. They are printed in full in Dr Wiley's book referred to above.

'The Wanderer of Switzerland' first appeared in *The Iris* in 1806. A famous (or infamous) critique of the poem was published in the *Edinburgh Review* in 1807, and although it was a hostile attack, it served to project Montgomery into the public arena. Dr Wiley writes that, by 1850, thirteen editions of the poem had been printed in Britain as well as others in America. The same author succinctly outlines the historic content of the poem:

In 1806 England and France were still at war. Switzerland's independence had been virtually yielded to Napoleon and France in 1798 but it was not until 1803 that total French domination had been imposed. The Swiss had resisted and lost; and many of those who survived emigrated to neighbouring countries and in numbers to America with, in Montgomery's words, 'the view of establishing a Swiss colony in some unoccupied part of the far West'.

The poem was written to oppose the Napoleonic oppression of Switzerland, then a small and almost helpless state. The poet prefaces the work with a descriptive introduction: 'A Wanderer of Switzerland and his family, consisting of his wife, his daughter and her young children, emigrating from their country, in consequence of its subjugation by the French, in 1798, arrive at the cottage of a shepherd, beyond the frontiers, where they are hospitably entertained.' The rest of the poem is an account of the conversations in the shepherd's home and ends with an announcement that the Wanderer intends to escape the tyranny of France and settle in a remote area of America.

'The West Indies' is a poem intended to support the abolition of slavery. Like 'The Wanderer', it deals with the theme of freedom. Southey thought the work lacked a unity normally found in Montgomery's verse. To quote Dr Wiley again, 'The sweep of the poem is vast, stretching from the discovery of Columbus to a vision beyond Montgomery's own present. Yet the variety of the landscapes prevents monotony ...'

Montgomery, in his introduction, writes, 'Written in Honour of the Abolition of the African Slave Trade, by the British Legislature in 1807'. The poem was composed on request in that year and published one year later. The poem ends on a note of optimism borne along by the writer's faith in the mercy of his Father in heaven.

Nor in the Isles and Africa alone,
Be the Redeemer's cross and triumph known:
Father of Mercies! Spread the promised hour;
Thy kingdom come with all-restoring power,
Peace, virtue, knowledge spread from pole to pole,
As round the world the ocean-waters roll! ...

And the last words of this emotive work:

Man, rising from the ruins of his fall,
Is one with God, and God is All in All.

The third of the quintet of longer works has the title 'The World before the Flood'. This is a poem which may properly be called 'religious'. In the original Preface to the poem (dated 1813), Montgomery wrote, 'There is no authentic history of the world from creation to the deluge, besides that which is found in the first chapters of Genesis.' This work, then, has a biblical origin and is built around an appeal to human conscience. The purpose is to use what Scripture is available in the 'book of origins' and to weave a narrative declaring, 'Truth in the Spirit though not in the letter'. The story is told as a parable only; and its value must be determined by its moral, or rather its religious, influence on the mind and on the heart. As would be expected, the poem ranges from the calamity of the fall to the coming of the King of Glory. The poet cannot refrain from the end note of pure worship.

Hail to the Day-Spring! Dawning from afar,
Bright in the east I see his natal star:
Prisoners of hope! Lift up your joyful eyes;
Who is this King of Glory from the skies;
Who is this King of Glory?—Mark his birth;
In deep humility he stoops to earth,
Assumes a servant's form, a Pilgrim's lot,
Comes to his own, his own receive him not,
Though angel-choirs his peaceful advent greet,
And Gentiles worship at his feet.

As for Milton, so with Montgomery: paradise was lost, but then found again in the coming of Messiah.

'Greenland' was written in 1818 as a tribute to the Moravian missionaries who had pioneered evangelism in the frozen Arctic regions. The poet explains his purpose like this:

The original plan was intended to embrace the most prominent events in the annals of ancient and modern Greenland;—incidental descriptions of whatever is sublime or picturesque in the seasons or scenery; … with a rapid retrospect of that moral revolution which the Gospel has wrought among these people, by reclaiming them, almost universally, from dark idolatry and savage ignorance.

Dr Wiley comments that Montgomery's interest in Greenland and the missionary endeavour there stemmed from his Fulneck days, and that appeals were made through *The Iris* for funds to support the Moravian work in the far north. The first three Moravian missionaries to Greenland were the famous Christian David and his two younger companions, Matthew and Christian Stach. Here, in a particularly poignant section, is the poet's eloquent tribute to Christian David.

Lo! on the deck with patriarchal grace,
Heaven in his bosom opening o'er his face,
Stands CHRISTIAN DAVID; venerable name!
Bright in the records of celestial fame,
On earth obscure; like some sequester'd star,
That rolls in its Creator's beams afar,
Unseen by man; till telescopic eye,
Sounding the blue abysses of the sky,
Draws forth its hidden beauty into light,
And adds a jewel to the crown of night …

Love—God's own love in his pure breast enshrined;
Love—love to man the magnet of his mind;
Sublimer schemes maturing in his thought
Than ever statesman planned or warrior wrought;
While, with rejoicing tears, and rapturous sighs,
To heaven ascends their morning sacrifice.

The last of the longer poems has the intriguing title 'The Pelican Island'. It was written in 1827 at the height of the poet's powers of descriptive verse. It relates an imaginary visit to some south-sea coral islands where the pelican 'is hatched, lives and dies'. It was the beauty and freedom of these unusual birds which fascinated Montgomery.

But it was not only the birds and the wildlife, but also the geological formation of the coral reefs that inspired the poet. Dr Wiley comments, 'The poem … draws on Montgomery's interest in art, archaeology, anthropology, the Bible, and philosophy.' Although there is no direct reference in the poem to the book of Genesis, the narrator uses parabolic method to move from creation, through development, to the ultimate mysteries of life and death:

O thou that readest! take this parable
Home to thy bosom; Think as I have thought,
And feel as I have felt, through all the changes
Which Time, Life, Death, the world's great actors wrought,
While centuries swept like morning dreams before me,
And thou shalt find this moral to my song:
Thou art, and thou canst never cease to be:
What, then, are time, life, death, the world to thee?
I may not answer; Ask Eternity.

Chronological profile

1734	John Montgomery (father) born
1742	Mary Blackley (mother) born
1768	John Montgomery and Mary Blackley m. in Ahoghill Parish Church, Ireland
1769	John and Mary Montgomery moved to Gracehill
1770	John (with Mary) Montgomery moved to Irvine, Scotland, as Moravian minister
1770	Mary Anne b. **19 April** (d. **6 August 1771**)
1771	James Montgomery b. **4 November** (d. **3 April 1854**)
1773?	Robert Montgomery (b. uncertain date)
1776	Ignatius Montgomery b. 4 September (d. **28 April 1841**); John (and Mary Montgomery and family) returned to Gracehill from Irvine
1777	James Montgomery sent to Fulneck, Yorkshire, for education
1783	John and Mary Montgomery called to the West Indies as Moravian missionaries
1784	James Montgomery collected *A Little Volume of Sacred Poems*
1787	James Montgomery left Fulneck to work in Mirfield, Yorkshire
1789	Montgomery left Mirfield and travelled south to Wentworth and then to Wath-on-Dearne
1790–1791	James left Wath-on-Dearne and travelled to London; John and Mary Montgomery died
1791	Montgomery returned to Wath-on-Dearne; he obtained a post with the *Sheffield Register*
1794	Joseph Gales left for USA; Montgomery purchased the *Sheffield Register*, renaming it *The Iris*
1795	Sheffield riots and Montgomery imprisoned in York Castle
1796	Second imprisonment in York and convalescence in Scarborough
1801	Published the poem 'Hannah' in *The Iris*
1802	Montgomery, after a period of depression, began the search for a renewed faith in Christ
1806–1812	Renewal of spiritual life; published 'The Wanderer' (**1806**); 'The West Indies' (**1807**) and 'The World before the Flood' (**1812**)
1813	First speech on a public platform

Appendix 2

1814	Made a life member of the Sheffield Sunday School Union; applied for membership of the Moravian congregation at Fulneck
1815	Montgomery's only recorded appearance in a pulpit
1819	Montgomery collaborated with Thomas Cotterill, vicar of St Paul's, Sheffield, in the publication of *A Selection of Hymns and Psalms;* Published 'Greenland'
1821–1822	Pub. *Songs of Zion*, hymns based on the psalms; Death of Elizabeth Gales
1825	Relinquished the position of editor of *The Iris* after thirty years; Pub. *The Christian Psalmist, Hymns Original and Selected*
1827–1830	Bible and missionary tours; Wrote Introduction to edition of *Olney Hymns;* Pub. 'The Pelican Island'
1832	Sheffield cholera epidemic; Montgomery appointed chairman of the Board of Health
1835	Began revision of the Moravian hymn-book (completed **1845**) Received royal pension £150/annum
1836	Moved from The Hartshead to The Mount
1838	Death of Anne Gales Coronation of Queen Victoria
1841	Death of Ignatius Montgomery at Ockbrook Montgomery in Scotland
1842	Visit to Ireland
1853	Pub. *Original Hymns*, a collection of 355 hymns
1854	Death of James Montgomery, **30 April**; Public funeral, **11 May**

The world of James Montgomery

The following paper was written by Sarah Groves for the *Moravian History Magazine*, *James Montgomery Issue* (Spring 1994), and is here reproduced with permission. This paper gives an excellent summary of the political times in which Montgomery lived.

A full appreciation of James Montgomery is helped by some background information about life in England during his time. Montgomery was born during the reign of George III (1760–1820). George III was a popular king, well known for his interest in farming—Farmer George. During his reign the American colonies were lost, the French revolted, Napoleon became Emperor and the Industrial Revolution started.

In 1774 the War of American Independence began; it was finally won in 1783 after many British defeats.

France was the most powerful nation in Europe despite its defeats at the hands of the Duke of Marlborough and the Earl of Chatham. But the country was living under an outdated feudal system. The French system was attacked by Voltaire and Rousseau who had observed the American Wars of Independence. In 1789 revolution broke out in Paris and the nobility were executed by the guillotine. Society was upturned, and France became a republic. After internal disagreements by the revolutionaries, the ambitious general Napoleon Bonaparte seized power and made himself Head of State. In 1804 he named himself Emperor. Soon his expansionist policies brought him into conflict with Britain.

In 1805 the French fleet was defeated by Nelson at the Battle of Trafalgar. Despite this defeat, Napoleon had by 1809 an empire that included, as direct subjects or dependent states which spread from France, Spain, Holland, western Germany, part of Poland and most of Italy. Napoleon's onward march was only halted when his army had to retreat from Moscow; and then in 1815 he was defeated by the Duke of

Wellington and a combined British and Prussian army at the Battle of Waterloo.

The French Revolution had a profound effect on British political life. It horrified the ruling classes, and encouraged others to expect more liberties in Britain. By 1792 the Tory government was so worried that public meetings were banned, and the Act of Habeas Corpus was suspended. Some have argued that it was only the strength of the Nonconformist churches in Britain at the time that prevented a similar revolution taking place there.

During this period the Industrial Revolution got well under way. In 1769 Hargreaves invented the Spinning Jenny which operated several wool spinning machines at once; in 1775 Watt invented the steam engine. However, the machinery which was being developed had the effect of making production cheaper and causing mass unemployment. The enclosure movement forced many country people off the land and into the towns in search of work.

The working classes lived in misery; it took an 18-hour working day to get just enough money to keep from starving, and the working conditions were dreadful. If workers were unlucky they were paid with 'stuff' rather than money.

Riots were common and these were often put down with great cruelty. People literally starved to death. The Corn Laws allowed the government to place taxes on imported wheat to help support the price of home produce. But this had the effect of raising the price of bread, the staple food of the poor.

In 1807 the act abolishing the slave trade in British colonies was passed. By 1815 proper roads began to appear across the country, financed by tolls collected at turnpikes. In 1820 George IV was crowned but caused a national outcry when he refused to let Queen Charlotte into [Westminster] Abbey to attend the coronation. The first modern railway, the Stockton to Darlington line, was opened in 1825 and this spelled the beginning of the end for the stage-coach companies.

William IV reigned from 1830–1837. In 1832 the Whigs managed to get the Great Reform bill passed. This bill extended the right to vote to more people, and abolished pocket boroughs. In 1833 a Factory Act was passed that made it illegal for children under 9 to work in cotton or wool factories, and limited the hours to be worked by older children. The Act for the Abolition of Slavery in British colonies received Royal Assent in August 1833. The Municipal Corporations Act of 1835 reformed the elections for borough and town councils.

In 1837 Queen Victoria came to the throne; she married Albert of Saxe-Coburg in 1840. Income tax was re-introduced by the prime minister Sir Robert Peel in 1841, and the cost of living fell. 1845 was the year of the great potato famine in Ireland. Peel fell from office in 1846 over the troubles in Ireland. There was still a great divide between rich and poor and the years from 1840–1850 were known as the 'Hungry Forties'. Wages were still dreadfully low, and the Corn Law taxes were keeping bread prices high. The People's Charter was formed; the Chartists demanded the vote for all men over the age of 21 and the right to vote in secret. In 1848 there were rebellions of working people in many European capitals. A large march to London was stopped by the Duke of Wellington and his troops.

1851 was the year of the Great Exhibition in Hyde Park and in 1854 Britain went to war with Russia in the Crimean War.

S. Groves

Select bibliography

This bibliography, although by no means exhaustive, lists works which have been found helpful. It may be used as a guide to further reading and research.

Benson, L. F., *The English Hymn* (London: n.p., 1915)

Cook, F., *Our Hymn-Writers and their Hymns* (Darlington: Evangelical Press, 2005)

Cooper, J. and E., (eds.), *The Moravian History Magazine* (1994)—this was a special James Montgomery edition

Daniel, C. P., 'Stand Up and Bless the Lord: The Story of the Sheffield Christian Education Council', lecture (Sheffield, 1975)

Ellerton, J., (ed.), *Collected Writings on Hymnology* (n.p., 1896)

Ellis, S., *The Life, Times and Character of James Montgomery* (London: n.p., 1864)

Fries, A., *Customs and Practices of the Moravian Church* (Winston-Salem, NC: Moravian Board of Education and Evangelism, 1973)

Holland, J., and **Everett, J.,** *Memoirs of the Life and Writings of James Montgomery* (7 vols; London: Longman, Brown, Green, Longmans and Roberts, 1854–1856)—a work which is indispensable for a serious study of the life of Montgomery

Horder, W. G., *The Hymn Lover: An Account of the Rise and Growth of English Hymnody* (London: n.p., 1889)

Houghton, E. H., *Christian Hymn-Writers* (Bridgend: Evangelical Press of Wales, 1988)

Jefferson, H. A. L., *Hymns in Christian Worship* (London: Rockliff, 1950)

Julian, J., *A Dictionary of Hymnology* (London: n.p., 1892)

Linyard, F., and **Tovey, P.,** *Moravian Worship* (Nottingham: Moravian Church, 1994)

Manning, B. L., *The Hymns of Wesley and Watts* (London: Epworth, 1942)

McGonigle, H. B., *A Burning and a Shining Light: The Life of William Bramwell* (Sheffield: Moorley's/Wesley Fellowship, 2009)

Montgomery, J., *The Poetical Works of James Montgomery, Collected by Himself* (London: Longman, Brown, Green and Longmans, 1854)

——*The Christian Psalmist: or Hymns Selected and Original* (9th edn.; n.p., 1825–1846)

Newton, J., and **Cowper, W.,** *Olney Hymns* (London: n.p., 1779)

Nuelson, J. A., *John Wesley and the German Hymn*, trans. Theo Parry, Sydney Moore and Arthur Holbrook (Calverley: A. S. Holbrook, 1972)

Pagdin, G., 'James Montgomery', lecture (Sheffield, 1964)

Routley, E., *I'll Praise My Maker* (London: Independent Press, 1951)

Samuel, B., *Spiritual Songs for Zion Travellers* (Sheffield: n.p., 1803)

Select bibliography

Schmoller, T., *Letters from a Newspaperman in Prison* (Newcastle: Allenholme Press, 2002)

Strong, R., *The Moravians at Fulneck* (Fulneck: Fulneck Museum, 1993)

Telford, J., *The Methodist Hymn-Book Illustrated in History and Experience* (London: n.p., 1959)

Thompson, A., *Poetical Works of James Montgomery with Life* (London: Nelson, 1867)

Tolley, G., 'James Montgomery', lecture (Sheffield, 1999)

Watson, J. R., *The English Hymn—A Critical and Historical Study* (Oxford: OUP, 1999)—a classic and important study of hymnology

Wiley, G., *The Poems of James Montgomery, with Critical Introduction* (Sheffield: Hallamshire Press, 2000)—a rare and valuable introduction to the poetry of James Montgomery. (This can be obtained from its author, Dr George Wiley, at 112 Button Hill, Eccleshall, Sheffield, S11 9HJ.)

Index of places

A

Ahoghill   13, 14, 116
America   18, 21, 42, 53, 63, 111, 112
Ayrshire   13, 14, 15

B

Bala   56
Ballymena   13
Barbados   15
Barnsley   35, 46
Bath   59
Bedford   14
Belfast   44, 60
Bohemia   18
Bristol   14, 57, 58, 59, 61, 79
British Museum, London   34
Buxton   59, 63, 64

C

Calver Street Methodist Church,
   Sheffield   53
Canada   18
Canterbury   87
Castle Hill, Sheffield   42
Chadderton Hall, Manchester   70
Cheshire   55
Cholera Monument, Sheffield   79
Clay Wood, Sheffield   79
Covent Garden, London   34

D

Derby   10, 14, 47, 60
Derbyshire   59
Devon   58
Doncaster   45, 46

D (continued)

Dublin   60
Dundee   59
Dunstable   64

E

Eckington   40, 44, 62
Edinburgh   59, 79, 111
England   7, 18, 19, 20, 21, 30, 41,
         44, 48, 56, 59, 60, 61, 72, 80,
                               87, 111, 118
Epworth   17, 121
Exeter   57, 59

F

Fetter Lane, London   21
France   41, 44, 111, 112, 118
Fulneck   3, 7, 10, 13, 14, 15, 17, 20,
        21, 22, 24, 25, 26, 27, 28, 29,
        30, 31, 34, 40, 50, 51, 53, 55,
        58, 60, 61, 82, 83, 84, 86,
                             113, 116, 122

G

Georgia   20, 21, 77, 84
Glasgow   59
Gloonan   13, 14
Gracehill   7, 13, 14, 15, 20, 60, 116
Great Houghton   35, 39
Greenland   18, 113

H

Hackney   68
Halifax   59
Harrogate   59
Herrnhut   18, 21, 61, 91

Homer 24, 110

Homerton College 47

I

Ireland 7, 10, 13, 14, 15, 17, 50, 56, 60, 116, 117, 120

Irvine 15, 17, 59, 116

K

Kilmarnock 59

L

Labrador 18

Lake District 60

Leeds 79

Lincolns Inn, London 65

Little Houghton 35

Liverpool 20, 63

London 10, 14, 18, 21, 31, 33, 34, 35, 56, 57, 58, 61, 64, 65, 66, 67, 68, 79, 84, 116, 120, 121, 122

M

Manchester 47, 58, 59, 68, 69, 70, 79

Masborough 31, 67

Matlock 59

Mechanics Library, Sheffield 10, 76

Mirfield 28, 29, 30, 31, 116

Moravia 18

N

Newcastle 58, 59, 79, 122

Norfolk Street Chapel, Sheffield 50

Nottingham Castle 65

O

Ockbrook 14, 60, 61, 86, 117

Olney 8, 26, 90

P

Peace Gardens, Sheffield 87

Perth 59

Peterborough 87

R

Raleigh, North Carolina 42

Red Hill, Sheffield 53

Rochdale 69

S

Saxony 18, 19, 61

Scarborough 37, 47, 48, 49, 116

Scotland 13, 15, 17, 56, 59, 61, 116, 117

Sheffield 3, 4, 6, 7, 8, 9, 10, 19, 24, 26, 30, 35, 37, 39, 40, 41, 43, 45, 46, 47, 48, 49, 50, 52, 53, 54, 55, 61, 62, 63, 65, 66, 67, 68, 71, 75, 76, 78, 79, 80, 81, 82, 87, 90, 110, 111, 116, 117, 121, 122

Sheffield General Infirmary 61, 75, 76

Sheffield University 53, 79

South Africa 18

St George's Church, Sheffield 81, 82

St Paul's Church, Sheffield 87

Stirling 59

Stockport 59

Stratford-upon-Avon 60

Swathe Hall 35

Swinton 32

Index of places

T

The Hartshead, Sheffield   40, 44, 55, 62, 63, 117

The Mount, Sheffield   52, 62, 63, 81, 117

Thurnscoe   35

Tobago   15

W

Wath-on-Dearne   7, 30, 31, 32, 34, 35, 36, 45, 61, 116

Wentworth   30, 31, 32, 61, 75, 116

West Indies   15, 18, 72, 77, 112, 116

Woolwich   14

Y

York   20, 45, 46, 47, 58, 59, 60, 81, 87, 116

York Castle   20, 45, 47, 58, 116

Yorkshire   6, 7, 13, 15, 17, 21, 27, 30, 34, 35, 47, 51, 60, 116

A

Albert, Prince Consort	80, 120
Aston, Joseph	47, 68, 69, 70
Athorpe, Colonel R. A.	45, 46, 48

B

Bennett, George	59, 65, 66, 67, 68
Blackley, Mary	14, 116
Blackwell, John	54
Booth, General William	92, 107
Bradley, Job	23
Bramhall, Mr	32, 33
Bunyan, John	60, 103
Burns, Robert	26, 57
Byron, Captain	35

C

Carey, William	77
Cennick, John	7, 13, 14, 50, 85
Chantry, Sir Francis	65
Charles, Revd. Thomas	56
Clark, Charles	50
Conder, Josiah	64, 85, 89
Cooper, Bishop Joseph	86, 88, 121
Cotterill, Revd. Thomas	87, 117
Cowper, William	8, 26, 57, 84, 90, 121

D

Doddridge, Philip	84, 89
Dryden, John	24, 57

E

Ellerton, Revd. John	84, 87, 121
Everett, James	7, 17, 30, 32, 54, 58, 73, 121

F

Fitzwilliam, fifth earl	30, 31, 61, 75
Fox, Charles	73

G

Gales, Anne	40, 44, 63, 82, 117
Gales, Elizabeth	40, 44, 62, 117
Gales, Joseph	39, 40, 41, 42, 44, 53, 62, 63, 86, 116
Gales, Sarah	44, 63, 64, 80, 81, 82
Garrick, David	60
Gerhardt, Paul	19, 86
Greathead, Revd Samuel	64

H

Holland, John	7, 30, 32, 36, 54, 61, 69, 71, 73, 81, 82, 92, 121
Hunt, Joseph	30, 31, 32, 33, 39, 45
Huss, John (or Jan)	18
Hutchinson, Colonel	65

I

Ingham, Benjamin	21

J

Johnson, Dr Samuel	58

K

Kent, Duke of	80
Kingsley, Charles	74

L

La Trobe, Peter	59, 61
Lacey, Anthony	10, 74
Lockwood, Mr	28, 29

Index of names

Luther, Martin 18, 19, 104

M

Manning, Bernard L. 85, 121
Mansell, William 36
Milton, John 24, 57, 110, 113
Molther 27
Montgomery, Bernard L., Viscount
  Montgomery of Alamein 13
Montgomery, Harriet 14, 80
Montgomery, Mary, née Blackley 14,
  15, 116
Montgomery, Revd Ignatius 14, 15, 35,
  51, 56, 57, 61, 65, 80, 82, 116, 117
Montgomery, Revd John 13, 14, 15,
  20, 116
Montgomery, Robert 14, 61, 116

N

Naylor, Benjamin 43, 48
Nelson, Lord 64, 118
Newton, John 72, 84, 90, 121

P

Paine, Thomas 31
Parken, Daniel 64, 65, 73
Pope, Alexander 24, 57
Pye Smith, J. 46, 47

R

Reynolds, Sir Joshua 58, 60
Roberts, Samuel 73
Routley, Erik 85, 121

S

Sangster, Revd Dr William· 104
Schmoller, Tanya 37, 46, 48, 122
Scott, Sir Walter 57
Shakespeare, William 57, 60
Smith, Matthew 54
Southey, Robert 73, 112

T

Tolley, Canon Dr George 3, 9, 10, 35,
  39, 53, 82, 87, 122
Toplady, Augustus 89
Turner, Hannah 35, 36
Tyerman, Revd Daniel 67

V

Vaughan, Felix 48
Vernon-Harcourt, Archbishop 87
Victoria, Queen 80, 117, 120
Virgil 24, 110

W

Walker, Joshua 67
Watteville, Bishop Johannes de 26
Watts, Isaac 3, 6, 84, 85, 89, 90, 92,
  103, 121
Wesley, Charles 3, 6, 7, 17, 21, 27,
  58, 84, 85, 89, 90, 121
Wesley, John 7, 18, 20, 21, 26, 27,
  58, 73, 77, 84, 121
Whitefield, George 7, 18
Wilberforce, William 72, 73
Wordsworth, William 26, 57, 73

Z

Zinzendorf,
Count Nikolaus Ludwig von   18, 19,
20, 21, 26, 61, 86, 94

About Day One:

Day One's threefold commitment:

- To be faithful to the Bible, God's inerrant, infallible Word;
- To be relevant to our modern generation;
- To be excellent in our publication standards.

I continue to be thankful for the publications of Day One. They are biblical; they have sound theology; and they are relative to the issues at hand. The material is condensed and manageable while, at the same time, being complete—a challenging balance to find. We are happy in our ministry to make use of these excellent publications.

JOHN MACARTHUR, PASTOR-TEACHER, GRACE COMMUNITY CHURCH, CALIFORNIA

It is a great encouragement to see Day One making such excellent progress. Their publications are always biblical, accessible and attractively produced, with no compromise on quality. Long may their progress continue and increase!

JOHN BLANCHARD, AUTHOR, EVANGELIST AND APOLOGIST

Visit our website for more information and to request a free catalogue of our books.

In the UK: www.dayone.co.uk
In North America: www.dayonebookstore.com

COLIN HAMER

160PP, ILLUSTRATED PAPERBACK

978-1-84625-083-5

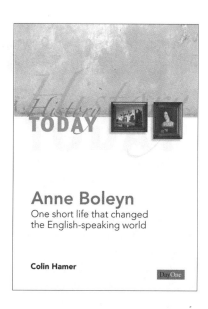

Anne Boleyn
One short life that changed
the English-speaking world

Colin Hamer

Anne Boleyn, twenty years old, stepped onto the shore at Dover in the winter of 1521 after several years abroad. She had been sent to France to assimilate French culture, and had used the time well. She was all set to make a big impression at the Tudor court—and did, capturing the heart of Henry VIII.

But this woman, who was in the grave by the age of thirty-six and on the throne of England for only three years, provokes strong reactions from many. Was she an immoral woman who seduced Henry away from his rightful wife for the advancement of family and personal gain? In this well-researched, fresh look at Anne, Colin Hamer sets her in her context as a young woman who had come to true faith in Christ, and shows the impact for good she made from her position of influence, an impact we still benefit from today.

Colin Hamer is currently chairman of a charity that works with the homeless and other vulnerable groups. Following his graduation from Liverpool University in 1972 with BA (Hons), he spent a short time teaching then pursued a business career for more than twenty-five years. He has been an elder at Grace Baptist Church, Astley, Manchester, for twenty years.

He and his wife Lois have two adult children. His first book, *Being a Christian Husband—a biblical perspective,* was published by Evangelical Press in 2005.

'In this fascinating biography of her short life, Colin Hamer skillfully shows how God prepared Anne for this important work and used her to bring Reformed truth into the powerhouse of England.'
—*Kath Dredge, Further Education tutor and manager of Hall Green BookPoint, Haworth*

'Colin Hamer's Anne Boleyn is as exciting as fiction as it carefully makes its way through the historical and religious complexities of Henry VIII's England.'
—*David B. Calhoun, Professor of Church History at Covenant Theological Seminary, St Louis, Missouri*

Christmas Evans—
no ordinary preacher

TIM SHENTON

176PP, ILLUSTRATED PAPERBACK

978–1–84625–130–6

Christmas Evans—
no ordinary preacher
The story of the 'John Bunyan'
of Wales

Tim Shenton

DayOne

Christmas Evans (1766–1838) was described by D. M. Lloyd-Jones as 'the greatest preacher that the Baptists have ever had in Great Britain'. This remarkable one-eyed Welshman came from humble beginnings to exercise powerful preaching ministries throughout Wales, particularly in Anglesey and the North. In this thoroughly researched biography, Tim Shenton paints an honest picture of Christmas Evans, not excusing or overlooking his faults, but demonstrating how this gentle and humble man, who possessed the spirit of prayer to a remarkable degree, was used by God for the extension of his kingdom in Wales.

Tim Shenton is the head teacher of St Martin's School and an elder at Lansdowne Baptist Church, Bournemouth, England. He is married with two daughters. He has written twenty books, and researched extensively on church history, specializing in the eighteenth and nineteenth centuries. His published works by Day One include *Heroes of revival, Our perfect God, Jesus in Luke's Gospel* and two other selections of children's daily readings, expositional commentaries on some of the Minor Prophets, *John Rogers—Sealed with blood,* and *Opening up 1 Thessalonians.*

'In this fascinating biography of her short life, Colin Hamer skillfully shows how God prepared Anne for this important work and used her to bring Reformed truth into the powerhouse of England.'
—KATH DREDGE, FURTHER EDUCATION TUTOR AND MANAGER OF HALL GREEN BOOKPOINT, HAWORTH

'Colin Hamer's Anne Boleyn is as exciting as fiction as it carefully makes its way through the historical and religious complexities of Henry VIII's England.'
—DAVID B. CALHOUN, PROFESSOR OF CHURCH HISTORY AT COVENANT THEOLOGICAL SEMINARY, ST LOUIS, MISSOURI

**John Rogers—
sealed with blood**

TIM SHENTON

144 PAGES, ILLUSTRATED PAPERBACK

978-1-84625-084-2

John Rogers—
sealed with blood
The story of the first Protestant
martyr of Mary Tudor's reign

Tim Shenton

Day One

We in the west sorely need to craft a theology of martyrdom—it would put backbone into our proclamation and living, and help us remember brothers and sisters going through fiery trials even today in other parts of the world. Remembering men like John Rogers is a great help in the development of such a theology. From the foreword by Michael Haykin, Principal and Professor of Church History and Reformed Spirituality, Toronto Baptist Seminary, Toronto, Ontario

'Tim Shenton has produced yet another well-documented, gripping biography of a real hero of faith—John Rogers (d. 1555), renowned biblical editor and first Marian martyr. Follow Rogers's fascinating career from Antwerp to Germany, and back again to England, where he was arrested, remained steadfast under intense interrogation, and paid the ultimate price for confessing Christ. This is a great book about an important epigone; hopefully, Rogers will no longer be marginalized! Highly recommended for teenagers and adults.'
—*JOEL R BEEKE, PURITAN REFORMED THEOLOGICAL SEMINARY, GRAND RAPIDS, MICHIGAN*

'Shenton weaves a brilliant tapestry from original sources and introduces the reader to many compelling and complex personalities. Well-proportioned in its emphasis, this history will be a vital contribution to studies of Protestant martyrs in Queen Mary's reign.'
—*RANDALL J. PEDERSON, CO-AUTHOR OF 'MEET THE PURITANS'*